MACHINE APPLIQUÉ
FOR THE TERRIFIED QUILTER

MACHINE APPLIQUÉ
FOR THE TERRIFIED QUILTER

SHARON PEDERSON

CREDITS

President & CEO Tom Wierzbicki

Publisher Jane Hamada

Editorial Director Mary V. Green

Managing Editor Tina Cook

Technical Editor Ellen Pahl

Copy Editor Melissa Bryan

Design Director Stan Green

Production Manager Regina Girard

Illustrator Laurel Strand

Cover & Text Designer Shelly Garrison

Photographer Brent Kane

MISSION STATEMENT

Dedicated to providing quality products
and service to inspire creativity.

Machine Appliqué for the Terrified Quilter
© 2008 by Sharon Pederson

That Patchwork Place® is an imprint of
Martingale & Company®.

Martingale & Company
20205 144th Ave. NE
Woodinville, WA 98072-8478 USA
www.martingale-pub.com

Printed in China
13 12 11 10 09 08   8 7 6 5 4 3 2 1

Library of Congress Cataloging-in-Publication Data is available upon request.

ISBN: 978-1-56477-820-8

DEDICATION

To my two "forever friends," Mary Ellen McQuay and Kathleen Shoemaker

ACKNOWLEDGMENTS

Many people contributed to the making of this book, some of them without even being aware of it. Everybody who asked how it was going and then offered encouragement is much appreciated, as are those who quietly but consistently make me aware of their support and friendship. With this, my fifth book, I have had more than my usual "cast of thousands" standing behind me cheering, led as always by my husband, Sy. Thank you, thank you, thank you for reminding me how lucky I am.

Specifically I would like to thank a group of talented quilt artists who have generously shared their work with me—and you—by allowing their quilts to be used as projects in the book. In alphabetical order they are: Diane Boyko, Judie Hansen, Gail MacRae, and Carol Seeley. Thanks also to Terre from Texas for her wonderful border technique.

To the wonderful Martingale gang—needless to say I couldn't do it without you, but, more important, I *wouldn't* do it without you.

CONTENTS

PREFACE

When I started quilting in the mid-1980s, I was strongly attracted to appliqué quilts. My attempts to create them by hand, however, were so abysmal that I gave up. For many years I referred to appliqué as "the A word." Of course my friends who remember that period of my life take great delight in reminding me of it, now that I am so passionate about machine appliqué. That's just what it took to make me a convert—learning that I could do it by machine. I should probably show you my logo so you know my feelings about hand work right off the bat.

It isn't that I don't appreciate handwork; I just don't want to do it. So, if you agree that life is too short to do hand work, this is the book for you.

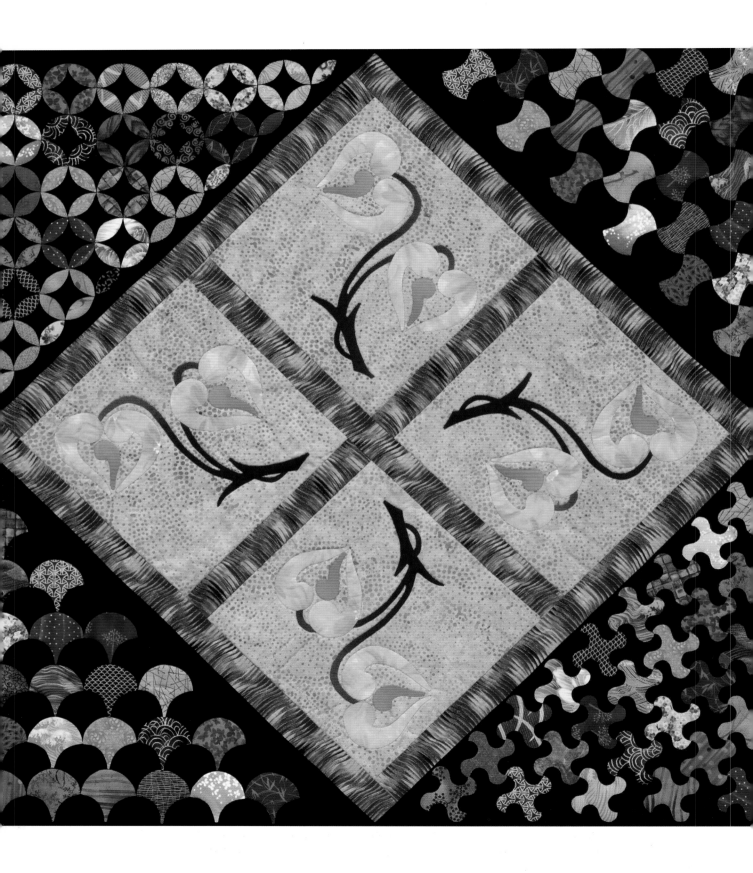

INTRODUCTION

What is appliqué, anyway? *The Oxford English Dictionary* defines it as "cut-out ornamental fabric sewn or fixed to the surface of another fabric." Interestingly, it does not mention whether the sewing is done by hand or machine, does it? Now that we've established the basic definition of appliqué, I will fill more than 100 pages showing you some of the many ways you can do it.

I separate appliqué into two broad categories. In the first, the edges are turned under and the thread doesn't show. In the second, the edges are not turned under and the thread may or may not show. It can be quite visible, as with a satin stitch, to become an important part of the design, or it can be invisible.

Within the two categories there are many variations. When you are planning a quilt, it's very important to choose an appliqué method appropriate for the end use of the quilt. For instance, if you are making a quilt for a small child, the appliqué had better be firmly attached or after the first dozen or so washings the whole thing will fall apart. Some of the more delicate variations of machine appliqué wouldn't be a good choice. Within the wonderful array of techniques presented, I'm sure you'll find the right one for whatever project you choose.

It is worth mentioning that you can mix the various types of appliqué in one quilt. If you start with invisible machine appliqué, that doesn't mean you can't throw in some fused sections or some reverse appliqué if that is the best way to achieve the look you want.

My approach to quilting is that I try very hard to find the easy way. This does not necessarily mean the fast way; as a matter of fact, some of my quilts take quite a while to make, but the overall process is easy and stress free. To ensure that I don't have to do things I don't like (which include hand work, basting, struggling with a large quilt through the small opening of my sewing machine, and paying a long-arm quilter to quilt my work), I make many of my quilts in small, manageable blocks. I do the piecing, appliqué, and quilting, and then I sew the blocks together using sashing strips. The method of making reversible blocks has been covered in my first two books, *Reversible Quilts* and *More Reversible Quilts*. Even if you don't plan to make your quilt reversible or have anything fancy on the back, it's a very efficient way to put a quilt together. It eliminates basting and allows you to work with the feed dogs up on your machine. (Yes, that means you don't have to work in a free-motion manner if you don't want to.) I'll provide more details on this method later.

We don't always make large quilts, however, and many of the quilts in this book are small. I figure that you bought the book because you might be just a little bit "terrified" about the prospect of machine appliqué, so why further terrorize yourself by trying a queen-size project first? This does not mean you can't machine appliqué a king-size quilt if that's what you want to do. But if you are just starting out, there are some nice little projects for you to tackle that won't require a major investment of either time or materials. Then, after you discover how easy it all is, you can move it up a notch and go fearlessly into the wonderful world of machine appliqué.

So, dive right in. Pick a project and try it out. What have you got to lose?

STARTING OUT—OR, THE TOOLS YOU NEED FOR THE JOB

As with any endeavor, the right tools make the job go more smoothly. For machine appliqué, you'll need all the standard equipment that you use for quilting, along with a few specific items that are covered in this section.

THE SEWING MACHINE

In a book about machine appliqué, perhaps the first thing we should discuss is the sewing machine. Many kinds of appliqué can be done with a basic zigzag sewing machine. When the stitch is intended to be invisible, it is hard to tell what kind of machine did the stitching. However, when the thread is highly visible, as with the satin stitch, there is a big difference between the satin stitch done on a $3,000 machine and a $300 one. Many years ago it was the inability to do a good satin stitch that had me shopping for a better machine, and I made sure before I left the store that my new machine would deliver.

There are things you can do that will improve your satin stitch, but if you have a machine that simply does not execute a good one, nothing you can do and no amount of practice will make up for the machine's deficiencies. At this point you must think like a man—go out and buy the right tool to do the job, and if that means a new sewing machine, go for it. Would *he* hesitate?

OK, now that we have that out of the way, let's talk about the things that you *can* do to help your machine give you the best possible stitch.

Keep your machine cleaned and oiled. Refer to the manual to see where the oil is to be applied, and make a habit of cleaning the lint out of the bobbin case on a regular basis. Get your machine professionally tuned up at least annually and more often if you are a heavy user. You wouldn't dream of neglecting the maintenance on your car, and today's machines are sophisticated pieces of equipment that deserve the same type of careful attention.

MACHINE FEET

The two feet I use most often when doing any kind of appliqué are the open-toe embroidery foot and, if I'm working through a quilt sandwich, the walking foot.

The open-toe embroidery foot gives you excellent visibility as there is no metal bar between your eye and the needle when sewing. Also, the bottom of it has an indentation, or groove, that glides over the heavy buildup of thread when doing a satin stitch.

SEWING-MACHINE NEEDLES

When I first started getting serious about machine work I looked at the array of needles available and thought (because to the naked eye they all looked pretty much the same), why do I need all those fancy things? Surely I can buy just one and it'll do. Boy, was I wrong. My initial results were far from acceptable, so I started doing some research about the whole needle thing. At the time it wasn't terribly easy to find information about needles, but now we have it at the touch of a mouse. There are Web sites that offer incredible amounts of needle information—just do an Internet search for "sewing-machine needles" and have a look. My favorite is the booklet "A Thread of Truth," available from the YLI Web site (www.ylicorp.com). It is packed with useful information about threads and both hand and machine needles. There are also many quilting books that explore in detail the various needles and why we should be using them.

Briefly, every specialty needle makes doing a particular task easier. For instance, if you are using embroidery threads, the embroidery needle with its large eye and special scarf designed to protect fragile threads would be the perfect choice. Similarly, the Metallica needle, made by Schmetz, has a special coating that makes it easier for metallic threads to glide through the eye without breaking.

MY CHOICE FOR INVISIBLE MACHINE APPLIQUÉ

One machine needle has gotten bad press lately, but I think it's indispensable for invisible machine appliqué. It's the universal needle. It was designed to allow the home sewer to avoid switching back and forth between a ball-point-type needle when sewing knits and a Sharp needle when sewing woven fabrics. The Sharp point would, of course, pierce a fiber and cause a run in the knit fabric. So, the universal needle was designed to be not as sharp as the Sharp needle nor as rounded as the ballpoint, and for general sewing it's fine. If you want to sew something that requires absolute precision though, the universal needle is going to disappoint you, because it will not pierce a fiber and therefore can't sew a perfectly straight line. When it hits a fiber, it is diverted ever so slightly to either the left or the right. The advantage is that the stitching doesn't leave a row of permanent holes—often the first clue that something has been machine appliquéd. What could be more invisible than a needle that does not leave permanent holes? For that reason, I choose the universal needle when doing invisible machine appliqué.

MACHINE NEEDLE SIZES

One thing all sewing-machine needles have in common is a size designation, which is indicated on the package by numbers that look like this: 60/8, 70/10, 80/12, and so on. The first number tells you that the needle is .6 or .7 or .8 of a millimeter (mm) thick, and the second number tells you much the same thing but without the use of the metric system. This means that a size 12 needle, unlike a size 12 dress that varies in size depending on the manufacturer, is always .8 mm thick. You know that .8 mm is bigger than .7 mm, so, as you can see, the numbers get bigger as the needle size increases.

Why do we have to worry about what size the needle is? Because you need to match the size of the thread you are using to the size of the needle to get good results.

The sewing-machine needle has a groove down the front, and the thread should fit into that groove. The needle makes a hole in the fabric and the thread should fill that hole; if the thread is too thick, it will drag and cause a puckered seam. The reverse scenario isn't good either. If the needle is too big, the thread (which passes back and forth through the eye of the needle an estimated 50 to 60 times before it becomes a stitch) can flutter and fray, and ultimately break.

So how are we supposed to know which thread fits which needle?

THREAD

Before we can work out the question I just posed, we need to discuss thread sizes. Let's do it using cotton thread that is sized using the English numbering system, as indicated on the spool by the letters Ne.

Very simply, a 1-pound weight was put on a scale and skeins of the same-size thread were piled up on the other side of the scale. When they balanced, the skeins were counted. If there were 60 skeins on the scale, that became 60-weight thread. So, if it took only 50 skeins to equal a pound, you know that it was thicker thread. As the number gets bigger the thread gets finer, which is, of course, the opposite of needle sizing.

Many spools of cotton thread include a second number that tells you how many plies of thread there are. So, 50/2 is 50-weight thread made up of 2 plies. The higher the ply number, the stronger the thread, so if you want more strength you would choose 50/3.

NEEDLE AND THREAD CHART

To make it easier to determine which threads are appropriate for each needle, I made a helpful little chart. I bought four spools of cotton thread in the sizes I use most often (60/2, 50/3, 40/3, 30/3) and one spool of invisible nylon thread (size .004). I typed needle sizes at the top of the chart and thread sizes at the bottom. I cut a piece of thread from each spool and taped it to the appropriate spot on the chart. Now I know at a glance which size needle fits each of the five weights of thread.

This chart is also helpful when I want to switch to another fiber, such as metallic or rayon thread, which is sized using numbers that do not correspond to cotton sizes. I compare the size of the other fiber to the size of the cotton threads on the chart, and I know what size needle to use.

The chart is only a starting point. For every project, particularly if I'm using a new thread, I test it on a piece of the fabric I will be using. If an 80/12 needle is too small for the thread, even though it looked right on the chart, I go up one needle size to see if I get better results.

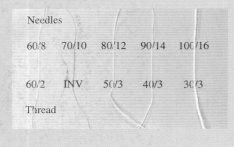

Needles				
60/8	70/10	80/12	90/14	100/16
60/2	INV	50/3	40/3	30/3
Thread				

BOBBIN THREAD

For invisible machine appliqué I use a neutral-colored 50/3 cotton thread in my bobbin. Medium gray is my favorite.

If you are seeing bobbin thread on top of your appliqué pieces and you can't get rid of it by loosening your upper tension, I would recommend matching the color of your bobbin thread to the appliqué fabric.

For satin-stitch appliqué you will be going through lots of bobbin thread, so a finer thread will help because you can wind more of it on your bobbin. There are special bobbin threads available, and a favorite of mine is Lingerie & Bobbin thread from YLI. It is 100% nylon and comes on 1,200-yard cones in two decorator colors—black and white. Another one from YLI is Soft Touch, which is a 60/2 cotton and comes on a 1,000-yard cone in the popular neutral colors of white, natural, gray, and black. Soft Touch is also available (in 24 additional colors) in 250-yard spools.

TAPE

Instead of using pins to hold the appliqué pieces in place, I rely on ordinary bargain-priced invisible tape. I find that the action of putting a pin through the appliqué piece moves it from where you want it to be, particularly with little pieces that have freezer paper underneath them. So, I tape the pieces in place and, when I come to a strip of tape, I remove it and "park" it on a piece of clear acrylic right beside my sewing machine. Then when I go back to my light box to prepare more appliqué shapes, I take along the piece of clear acrylic with all the tape segments stuck to it and use them over again.

Another indispensable feature of tape is its ability to hold things down while still allowing you to see where you're sewing. When I have sharp points to sew, I leave the tape in place and sew right through it. I'm sure you've had the experience of trying to appliqué a very sharp point and finding that when the needle comes up, it lifts the point with it. Sewing through tape eliminates this problem. Remember to remove all the tape when you finish sewing, and whatever you do, don't iron it. (Ask me how I know about that—or, on second thought, don't!)

FRAY CHECK

There are some situations in appliqué when you can't get quite the width of seam allowance you would like; this is when a bottle of Fray Check comes in handy. It is a clear liquid that you paint on with the handy little applicator tip on the bottle. As the name implies, it helps keep those tiny little seam allowances from fraying. It dries quickly and does not stain. If you are concerned about a particular fabric, do a test on a scrap first to see if it causes any discoloration.

FABRIC

I use 100%-cotton fabric almost all the time. Occasionally I'll find something else that I want to work with, but only when I'm trying to achieve a very special effect. I used to wash all my fabrics before using them, but now I only wash the ones that I'm worried might run or shrink. We are so blessed with the quality of quilting-weight cottons that are available to us. My advice is to shop only at reputable, independent quilt shops where you know you are going to get good quality and good service.

BATTING

My all-time favorite is Hobbs Heirloom Cotton, which is 80% cotton and 20% polyester, but the newer Hobbs Fusible Heirloom Cotton is taking over first place for me. It is so handy having the ability to fuse your backing, batting, and top together (the glue comes out the first time you wash your quilt), and if you have to separate the three layers for any reason, they come apart with a gentle pull. You can then fuse them again if necessary.

LIGHT BOX

A light box is made of a clear, hard surface (acrylic or glass) with a non-heat-producing lightbulb underneath it. On it you can place your pattern, cover it with freezer paper, and see the pattern easily. Similarly, you can put your background fabric on top of a placement diagram on your light box and, with the light shining through it, readily see where each appliqué piece goes.

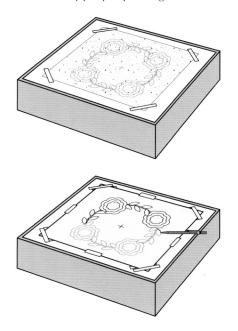

My light box never gets put away. I use it often, particularly when doing appliqué, as it provides the easiest way to line up appliqué pieces accurately. If you have a clear acrylic extension table for your sewing machine, you can put one of those small fluorescent lights (such as an Ott Light) under it to make a very good substitute for a light box. A clear glass table with a lamp underneath it will also work.

THE BROOKLYN REVOLVER

No, we aren't using firearms—we're using the handiest little tool that you will become very fond of when cutting, gluing, and turning under seam allowances on hundreds of leaves or whatnot.

One side can be used as a cutting mat, and the other side can be ironed on. It revolves like a lazy Susan and when you are doing something repetitive, such as gluing lots of little pieces, it helps keep them in place. Instead of having to move each little piece, you simply rotate your wonderful Brooklyn Revolver. (See "Resources" on page 110.)

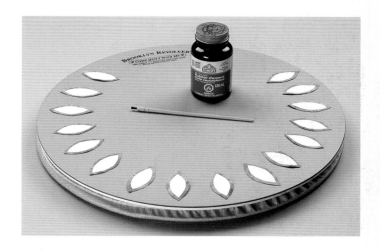

INVISIBLE MACHINE APPLIQUÉ

In this method, which is sometimes referred to as mock hand appliqué, we will turn under the edges of our appliqué motifs and stitch them down with a stitch that, while strong, is not going to be a distracting element. I like to use a basic zigzag stitch. I know that many machine appliquérs like the blind hemstitch, but when I look at that stitch I see four or five stitches that seem pointless and then one zigzag stitch that holds the appliqué piece. What do those four or five stitches actually do? Nothing, as far as I can see.

Blind hem stitch

THE INVISIBLE ZIGZAG STITCH

I start by setting my machine to the narrowest possible zigzag. You must be able to see the needle moving from right to left—on my machine the width setting is .5, on some machines it is .6. I set the length to 2.5. This is what it looks like.

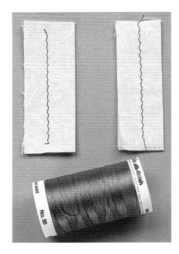

Stitch width on the left is .5;
width on the right is .6. Stitch length is 2.5 for both.

Stitch a practice piece to get the settings right on your machine. Start with the width at .5 and the length at 2.5. Using a sample of the appliqué and background fabrics you will be working with, start with the needle in the right position at the very edge of the appliqué fabric. It should be so close that the shaft of the needle touches the appliqué while the point is in the background fabric. When the needle swings to the left it should just catch the very edge of the appliqué fabric. This way only the stitches to the left are actually on the appliqué and the thread just disappears along the edge.

Be careful to keep only the left stitch on the appliqué (as on the right side of the appliqué above) or it will not be invisible. If you end up with both the zig and the zag on the appliqué (as on the left side of the appliqué above), the thread will show and the appliqué piece will take on a kind of topstitched look.

Visibility is a major issue here. You must be able to see the needle moving from right to left so that you can guide the fabric through the machine. If you can't see the needle moving from right to left, increase the width until you can.

ADDITIONAL MATERIALS

There are a few more supplies you'll need for this type of machine appliqué. They are readily available and inexpensive.

Freezer paper. This is one of the handiest items in an appliquér's toolbox. It comes in rolls that are 18" wide and you can buy it at the grocery store. If in doubt, look for the words plastic or poly-coated on the box. It is *not* waxed, and if you accidentally get waxed paper, all of your work will be in vain because it doesn't stick to fabric when ironed. Waxed paper melts, leaving an ugly wax stain.

Freezer paper has a shiny side and a dull one. You do all your drawing—in pencil only—on the dull side, and then you put the shiny side next to the wrong side of your fabric before ironing it in place. By pressing with a dry iron, you make your templates stick to the fabric, and if you don't like the placement you can peel the template off easily and reposition it.

Turning tool: For turning seam allowances, you'll want a comfortable tool such as a round toothpick, a bamboo stylus, or a smooth chopstick.

Rubber cement. I'm often asked, "Why rubber cement?" and I answer:

- Because it's cheap.
- It goes on easily and dries quickly.
- It stays flexible for years and years.
- It sticks only to itself, so when you get it on your fingers *you* don't stick to all your little appliqué pieces.
- It "lets go" easily when you want to remove the freezer paper from behind your appliqué pieces.

Purchase a bottle at your local hardware or stationery store (see the photo on page 15). Remember when working with rubber cement to have good ventilation, and when you lift the lid to get some on your brush, always set the cap back on straight so that fumes aren't escaping from the bottle into the room.

Purchase a dozen or so disposable paintbrushes and before using them give each one a "haircut." I find that the long bristles are too flexible and it's hard to control where the glue goes.

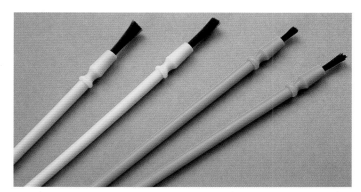

Shown here are disposable paintbrushes for use with rubber cement. The blue brushes have been trimmed.

USING RUBBER CEMENT

1. Using your trimmed paintbrush, apply a small amount of glue on both the freezer-paper template and the appliqué fabric; because rubber cement sticks only to itself, you must put glue on both pieces that are to be stuck together. Wait for it to dry—about one minute. When it is no longer shiny it is dry. This is not one of those adhesives that will be ruined if you don't position the pieces within 30 seconds. So, when the phone rings right in the middle of gluing something— don't worry, you can chat as long as you want and come back to your project when you're ready.

2. Using a turning tool, turn the seam allowance over onto the freezer paper. The glue will hold it in place but remain flexible for years and years, which means that if you have to peel it back to remove a little wrinkle or something you can do so easily.

3. If you are doing an area, such as a corner, where one layer of fabric will be turned over on top of another, you will need to apply a little glue to the fabric after turning the first seam allowance. Remember, rubber cement sticks only to itself, so if you cover the freezer paper with one seam allowance you have to apply additional glue before turning the second one.

Freezer paper

Add glue here before turning over seam allowance.

PREPARING THE APPLIQUÉS

1. Draw your appliqué pattern onto the dull side of the freezer paper with pencil only. Ink will mix with the rubber cement and make a huge mess. If making multiple copies of one pattern, layer up to three additional pieces of freezer paper underneath the one with the design drawn on it and staple them together. If there is a right and wrong direction to your appliqué, keep all the freezer-paper layers with the dull side up or you will be making mirror-image designs, which might not be what you want.

MARKING TRICK

If you are working with a template that will need to be centered onto the background or have something centered on top, use a thick needle to mark the center on the design, piercing all the layers at once.

2. Cut directly on the drawn line; do not add any seam allowance. Remove the staples.

3. Using a dry iron, iron the shiny side of the freezer paper to the wrong side of your appliqué fabric.

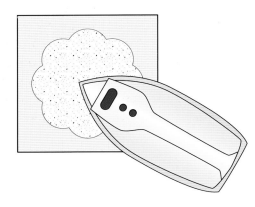

4. Cut around the appliqué pieces, leaving between ⅛" and ¼" for seam allowance. Clip inside corners and curves, but keep in mind that clipping weakens the appliqué, so do it sparingly. It's easy to add a clip when turning the seam allowance over, so if you're not sure an area needs it, wait until you turn that section.

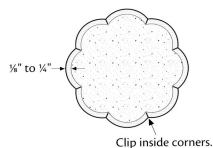

⅛" to ¼"→

Clip inside corners.

5. Apply a little bit of glue to both the freezer paper and the fabric, all along the seam allowance. I run the little brushes so that the edge of the paper is right down the middle of the brush. You are not gluing the entire seam allowance.

   Note: If working on a circular design it's a good idea to mark—with pencil—your starting point. I once found myself going around a circle for the second time because the glue had dried where I started and it's almost invisible when it dries.

Starting point

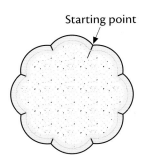

6. When the cement is dry, turn the seam allowance over using a round toothpick or a bamboo stylus. If it doesn't stick, you either did not put on enough glue or you didn't let it dry.

7. At every clipped point you have a weak spot, so I put a dab of Fray Check at those points before they get sewn down.

Add Fray Check.

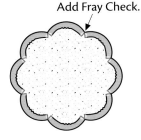

POSITIONING THE APPLIQUÉS

There are a number of different ways to get the pieces where you want them. An easy way is to just eyeball the placement—but I know that with some designs this isn't good enough.

Negative image. One of my favorite methods is to retain both the positive and negative images when cutting out templates—often the negative image is the perfect thing to use when placing the appliqué in position. I cut the image out of a square of freezer paper the same size as the background; then I can place the square on the background and quickly position the appliqué.

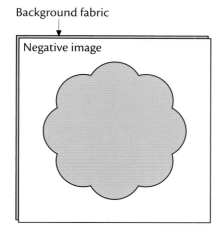

Background fabric

Negative image

Light box. Another useful tool is a light box (see illustration on page 15). If you put a placement diagram on the light box and cover it with the background fabric, you can easily see where to put the next petal or leaf. It helps if you mark the center of both the placement diagram and the background fabric and line them up each time you position an appliqué piece. For square shapes of either paper or fabric, find the center by folding in half in both directions.

Grid method. With some designs the easiest thing is to draw a grid on the background fabric, being careful to test your marking pencil first to make sure you'll be able to remove the marks. Three of the four corner designs on "Sashiko Revisited" (page 77) were done this way.

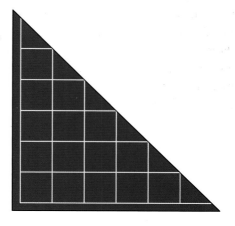

Once the pieces are positioned where you want them, tape them in place one at a time, and then sew.

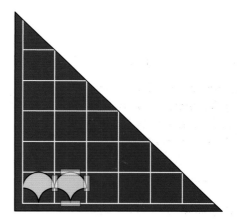

STITCHING THE APPLIQUÉ

Thread your machine with either 60/2 cotton thread that matches your appliqué piece, or invisible thread and a 60/8 universal needle. In the bobbin you should have a neutral-colored 50/3 cotton thread. Test your stitch length and tension on a practice piece. If you see the bobbin thread on the top, try loosening the upper tension or tightening the bobbin tension. If the thread still shows on top, match the bobbin thread to the appliqué fabric.

1. Anchor your stitches with about ³⁄₈" of tiny little straight stitches. I put them in an unobtrusive spot right up against the edge of the appliqué fabric. Change to a narrow zigzag stitch and stitch around your appliqué piece, pivoting as often as necessary.

2. When you reach the point where you started, change back to very small straight stitches and anchor the end of the stitching line.

3. Remove the piece from the machine and use sharp trimming scissors to cut away the excess fabric from the back, leaving ¼" seam allowance.

Trim ¼" inside stitching line,
exposing the freezer paper.

4. With a pointed, but not sharp, tool (such as smooth chopsticks, the blunt end of a bamboo stylus, or the ends of the disposable brushes), peel back the seam allowance at a straight part of your stitching and expose the edge of the freezer paper. Put the pointed tool under the freezer paper and move it around to release the paper from the appliqué fabric. Gently pull the freezer paper with one hand while holding the stitching line with the other. Don't worry if you rip the paper; however, if you can remove the template in one piece, you'll have the advantage of being able

to use it again. If you have difficulty getting the paper out, you probably used too much glue. Or, if the edge of the paper rips everywhere and the perforations from the sewing-machine needle are well into the paper, your stitch was probably too wide.

REVERSE APPLIQUÉ

What is the difference between appliqué and reverse appliqué? I think the name has caused all sorts of confusion when the reality is quite simple. We have already learned the definition of appliqué—that is, one fabric is sewn onto a different background fabric. So, if you sew a flower to a background fabric, that is appliqué. But what if it was easier to cut a flower-shaped hole in the background fabric and put the flower fabric behind? That is reverse appliqué, plain and simple. Instead of the flower fabric being on top, the background fabric is actually the top layer. Use the same stitching method for reverse appliqué as for regular appliqué.

I often choose to reverse appliqué if it makes what I want to do easier. Look at the examples below. Which would you rather do: appliqué the long, narrow points of the star, or reverse appliqué the background with its much easier points? I'd say go for the reverse-appliqué version—nobody can tell the difference from two feet away and even if they could, there's nothing wrong with finding the easier way to do the job. I used reverse appliqué in "Crazy Hearts" (page 33) and "Gail's Garden" (page 55).

The end results of reverse appliqué and regular appliqué are nearly identical, as evidenced by the top two samples. Reverse appliqué is shown on the left and traditional appliqué is shown on the right. Note that the star points of the reverse appliqué piece shown in the lower-left corner will be much easier to turn under than the points of the gold star shown in the lower-right corner.

FUSIBLE APPLIQUÉ

In "Invisible Machine Appliqué," we learned different ways of appliquéing that involve carefully turning under the edges before stitching them in place. In this section we will not be turning any edges under; rather, we will be adhering the appliqués to the background with fusible web. With this method, the thread can either be "invisible" or it can be a focal point. You may want to review the section about needles and thread beginning on page 12 before going on.

WORKING WITH FUSIBLE WEB

My favorite fusible product is Steam-A-Seam 2, made by the Warm Company (see "Resources" on page 110). This is the product I am referring to when I use the term *fusible* throughout the book.

Be careful when trying a new fusible-web product. They all come with instructions and I strongly recommend reading them carefully before using any product in a quilt. Don't assume that because one fusible requires 10 seconds of heat to fuse it, they all will. The setting on your iron may need to be different for different brands. If you don't use the product correctly, don't be surprised if you get poor results.

My advice is that once you find the fusible product that works best for you, learn its properties and you will always be able to count on the results if you follow the manufacturer's instructions.

Steam-A-Seam 2 is available by the yard or in 8½" x 11" sheets, which is the way I prefer to buy it. There are two lining papers, one on either side of the fusible web. Draw your appliqué patterns on the piece of paper that is most securely stuck to the fusible web. You don't want your pattern paper to fall off the fusible web before you get it cut out. A nice property of Steam-A-Seam 2 is that it will temporarily "stick" to the background fabric before fusing. It will stay put and not slide around while you are arranging other pieces.

The fusing process consists of five steps:

1. Draw or trace your design in reverse on the paper liner that is most securely attached to the fusible web. (The patterns in this book are already reversed for easy tracing.) I always use pencil, although there are no indications on the Steam-A-Seam package to suggest it's necessary. I feel that it is much easier to remove a bit of pencil mark from your fabric if needed than to remove ink.

2. Remove the paper liner that does *not* have your design drawn on it, and hand-press the exposed web to the wrong side of your appliqué fabric. Do *not* use an iron yet.

3. Cut through all layers—fabric, paper liner, and fusible web—on the drawn line. Do not add a seam allowance.

4. Peel off the remaining paper liner, making sure the web is attached to your fabric, and position the appliqué piece on your background fabric. If you are doing a piece with many interlocking parts, you can rearrange the pieces until you get them exactly right—the web is sticky enough to hold them in place. They do not become permanently affixed until ironed.

5. When you are absolutely certain you have the appliqué in the right place, iron for 10 to 15 seconds with the iron on the cotton setting (assuming you are using cotton fabric). If the piece is larger than the base of your iron, overlap pressed areas so that you don't miss any sections.

FOUNDATION PAPERS

When doing satin-stitch appliqué, it is necessary to have a foundation paper underneath the background fabric to help feed it smoothly through your machine. I particularly like the 8½" x 11" sheets called Fun-dation (see "Resources" on page 110). The sheets are made of 75% rayon and 25% polyester. They do not dull the sewing-machine needle, and they are easy to remove. A nice bonus is that they feed well through my computer printer and photocopy machine.

If you need to use more than one piece of foundation paper under a large appliqué piece, try not to overlap them. It's difficult to remove the paper later if there is more than one layer.

To test the effectiveness of foundation paper for yourself, fuse a piece of fabric to a background scrap and put a piece of foundation under only part of it. Set your machine to a satin stitch and start stitching over the area with the foundation paper under it. When you get to the end of the foundation paper, keep on stitching and watch what happens to the fabric. It draws up, creating a tunnel underneath and distortion on top. The wider the satin stitch is, the more obvious the tunneling becomes.

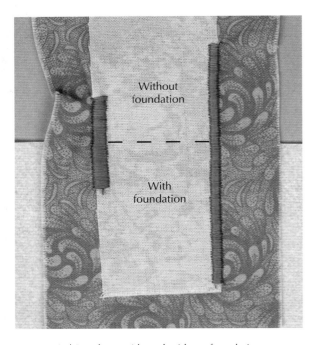

Satin stitching done with and without foundation paper

THE SATIN STITCH

In the section about sewing machines on page 12, I mentioned that some machines do not produce a good satin stitch. What you are looking for is a stitch that is consistent in both width and density. You do not want to see gaps between the stitches, nor do you want to see wobbly bits. I know that's a highly technical term, but believe me, that is the only way to describe some of the stitching I have seen in classes. We will assume you already have a machine that produces a good satin stitch or you have an appointment at your local sewing-machine store to get one that does. But first, let's go over the steps you should take to see what yours can do.

1. Fuse a piece of fabric to a background—any size or shape will do, as this is just to test your stitches. Put a piece of foundation paper underneath.

2. Thread your machine with a thread that contrasts with your appliqué fabric so you can easily see the stitches. Choose a 60/2 cotton thread and put a new 60/8 needle in your machine. Put the open-toe embroidery foot on your machine. (It's the one with the wide groove on the bottom.) That foot is essential when executing a satin stitch; without the groove underneath, the buildup of thread will occasionally cause the foot to hang up and the fabric will stop moving. Before you realize what's happened, the thread breaks. When you investigate you discover a horrible knot, and when you finally get it all picked out you have a hole in the fabric. This is not good.

Notice the groove on the bottom of the open-toe embroidery foot.

3. Fill your bobbin with either 60/2 cotton thread or 50/3 cotton thread in a neutral color. My favorite is medium gray. If your machine has the little hole at the end of the bobbin finger, thread the bobbin thread through it. This tightens your bobbin thread without requiring you to tighten the screw.

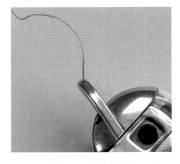

Bring thread through the hole at the end of the finger on the bobbin case.

4. Set your machine to a zigzag stitch and choose a medium width. If it's too narrow, you won't be able to see how good a job your machine is doing. If it's too wide, you'll use a whole spool of thread just testing your stitches.

5. Loosen the upper tension just a little. With the satin stitch, you want the upper thread to show a bit underneath; to accomplish that, you loosen the upper thread and sometimes tighten the bobbin thread. Always start with the upper tension, as it is the easier one to adjust. If you can't get it right without also adjusting the bobbin tension, the world as we know it will *not* end if you change the bobbin tension.

Note: I know that some of you will break out in a cold sweat if I even suggest touching the bobbin tension because somebody told you NEVER to do that. But, I'm going to ask you—what is there to be so skittish about? It's only a screw, which if turned ever-so-slightly to the left will loosen the tension and if turned to the right will increase the tension. Now, how hard is that? If you're concerned about not getting it back to where you had it originally, just picture the screw position as being like the hands on a clock. If it was at two o'clock when you started, make sure you return it to two o'clock when you're finished.

Screw is at two o'clock on the bobbin case.

6. Align the needle so that when it comes down to the right it is in the background fabric at the very edge of the appliqué piece. When the needle swings to the left, all the thread will be on the appliqué. You want your stitches to be at right angles to the edge of the appliqué (stitching in the diagrams is exaggerated for clarity).

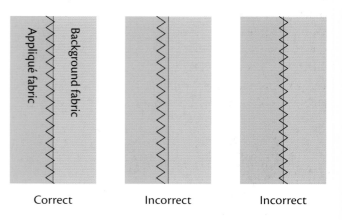

Correct   Incorrect   Incorrect

SEW STEADY

One very important requirement when doing satin stitching is to sew at an even speed—and don't go too fast. If you doubt me, do a test with an even, *moderate* speed, and then an even, *fast* speed, and compare the results. You'll find that you get a more consistent stitch when not trying to set the world land-speed record for sewing machines.

So, how does it look? Are you getting good coverage? If not, reduce the length of the stitch and try again. You want the thread to completely cover the appliqué fabric.

The stitch length is too long here. Shorten it until you can't see pink fabric between the stitches as in the lower section.

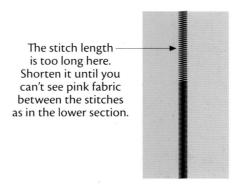

Can you see bobbin thread on the top? If so, loosen the top tension a bit, or tighten the bobbin tension a bit. When adjusting tension, always make changes in very small increments.

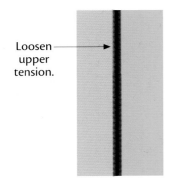

Loosen upper tension.

Keep testing until you achieve a width you like, with good coverage and no bobbin thread visible on top. Now we're ready to try some corners, curves, and points.

CORNERS, CURVES, AND POINTS

To practice stitching around curves, points, and right-angled corners, use the arrow pattern on page 27. Referring to "Working with Fusible Web" on page 21, prepare the arrow and fuse it to a background fabric. Thread your sewing machine with thread that will look good on your appliqué fabric, put the open-toe embroidery foot on the machine, and layer a foundation paper underneath your background fabric; you are ready to go.

Read the following sections on curves, inner and outer points, and right-angle corners as they relate to the stitching diagram below. Then start stitching at A and sew a sample, incorporating all you've learned. We will cover the different sections of the arrow as we come to them.

POINT A: STARTING AND STOPPING

When you start, you must first anchor your stitches. Set your machine to a straight stitch that is very closely spaced. Position the needle right at the edge of the appliqué with the needle in the background, and sew about 15 tiny little stitches (approximately ³⁄₈"). Switch to a zigzag stitch and continue sewing. When you reach the point where you started the zigzag stitch, switch back to a straight stitch, reposition the fabric so that the needle is right along the edge of the appliqué stitches, and anchor the end as before. Cut off the thread tail close to the anchoring stitches.

F

D   H

E

C

Pivot points   A
                      Start here.

B   Pivot points

Stitching diagram

CURVES

To keep your stitches at right angles to the edge of the appliqué when stitching curves, it is necessary to pivot. Where you pivot depends on whether you are stitching an inner or an outer curve.

When pivoting on an outer curve, pivot with the needle in the right, or outside, position. When pivoting on an inner curve, pivot with the needle in the left, or inner, position. If you pivot in the wrong place you will end up with little pie-shaped blank sections.

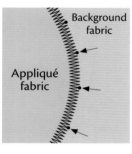 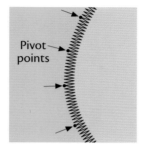

Outer curve   Inner curve

POINTS B AND C: RIGHT-ANGLE CORNERS

Once you've rounded the first curve on the arrow pattern, you'll come to the first of two right-angle corners. There are two ways to pivot and turn at these corners. Practice both to see which one you prefer. Do the first one at point B and the second at C.

1. The first method of stitching right angles is not my favorite, but it has its fans. When stitching toward the corner, stop with the needle in the right position, when the thread has covered the last thread of the appliqué fabric. Pivot and continue sewing. The second pass of zigzag stitches will be on top of the first stitches and will create a bit of a lump.

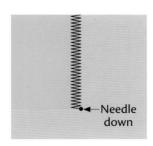 

2. Stitch until you reach the second right-angle corner (C), and stop with the needle in the left position, when the thread has covered the last bit of the appliqué fabric. Pivot, but if you continue stitching the needle will head to the right—into the background fabric—which you do not want. You must manipulate the needle and fabric, moving the fabric so that when the needle swings to the right it goes into the background fabric exactly where you want the next stitch to be. Essentially you follow the thread back into the hole it came out of. This does not give you a buildup of thread; the stitching, after you turn the corner, is not on top of the previous stitching.

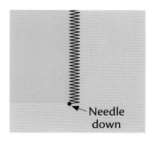 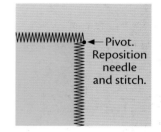

POINT D: INNER POINTS

After turning the C corner, you'll stitch an inner curve (don't forget to pivot with the needle in the left, or inside, position). Then we come to D, an inner point. As you are stitching on the line from C, approaching point D, stop and draw a line extending the line at D the width of your stitch. In the illustration this line is exaggerated for visibility.

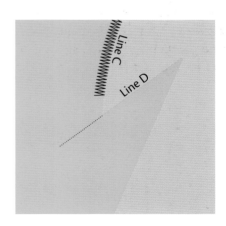

1. When you get to the inner point D, do not stop stitching. Continue until the needle, when in the left position, hits the line you have drawn. You will have as many as six or seven stitches beyond the point, depending on the width of your stitch.

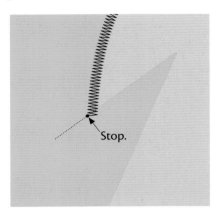

2. Pivot, but before you continue stitching (the needle is going to go to the right), manipulate the fabric so that when the needle goes in, it is following the thread and going into the hole it just came out of. That way you won't have a thread out in the middle of nowhere, ruining your appliqué. As you continue sewing, you will see that when the needle goes to the right it will be exactly at the edge of the appliqué—just where you want it to be.

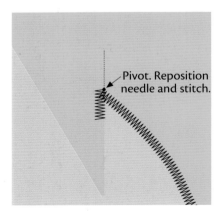

REMINDER

Be sure to sew up to the extension you drew at point D. If you pivot too soon on an inside point, you will have a blank spot.

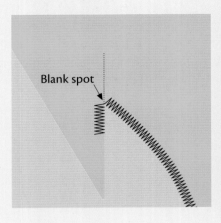

POINTS E AND F: OUTER POINTS

As you can imagine, there is more than one way to stitch a narrow point. I'm going to explain two methods—they are the ones I like best.

1. As you are approaching point E, watch the needle carefully. When it hits the left side of the appliqué fabric while going to the left, start decreasing your stitch width so that it continues to cover the edges of the appliqué fabric as it gets narrower. In effect, when the needle is in the left position it is on the left side of the point, and when it goes to the right it is on the right side of the point. You have to slow down when doing this or you'll be off the end of the point before you know it.

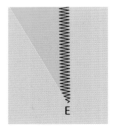

2. When you get to the point, pivot and carefully start increasing your stitch width until you get back to the width at which you started. It's a good idea to make a note of the width before you start decreasing.

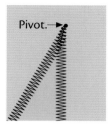

3. As you stitch past E, toward the next point, F, imagine a line dividing point F in half.

4. As you are stitching toward point F, begin to decrease the width of your stitch so that it stays inside that imaginary line. As you start decreasing, stitch very slowly, keeping an eye on the distance to the point and the width of your stitch. You don't want to get too narrow, as it will just peel threads off the outside of the appliqué piece. It's better to have the stitches overlap slightly at the point.

5. When you get to the point, pivot and increase your stitch width until you get back to the width at which you started. You should be increasing at the same point and at the same rate as you decreased when going the other way. In other words, both sides should look the same.

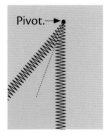

6. Continue stitching around the arrow. Stitch the outer point at G in the same manner as E or F. Stitch the inner point H in the same way as D. When you approach A, anchor your stitches again, and you're done!

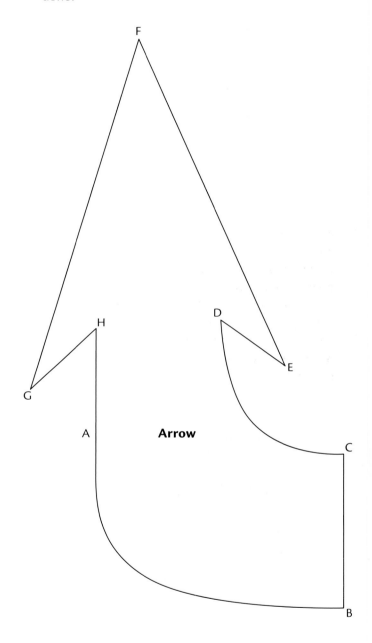

CREATING A MOOD

You can choose your stitch and thread color to match an emotion or establish a mood. This sample was a practice piece for a quilt I made for a friend who had suffered a broken heart. Being the kind of person who, if a man, would probably wear suspenders and a belt, I first did a practice piece for the "broken heart" part of the quilt to make sure the thread would create the feeling I wanted.

The small sample was done to check the tension, stitch width, and thread choices. The larger sample was done to determine the correct size and spacing of the scallop stitch.

When I had made my thread choices and I had the tension the way I wanted it, I did a full-sized sample to make sure I could get the little scallops around the larger heart to match perfectly. Once I had it all worked out, I made the quilt and sent it off.

To get the broken-heart look, I dropped the feed dogs and left the stitch set for zigzag. The machine still moves the needle from left to right, but it does not move the fabric forward through the machine. You get to do that, and it allows you to create some interesting effects, including the jagged broken-heart look that I wanted. Try dropping your feed dogs with your machine set to zigzag and just fool around. Think of other areas where you could use the technique—if you look at it sideways can you see flames? Grass? (Well, maybe if you change to green thread.)

What about a primitive look? I was trying to make the sample below look like a child had done it, so I wanted the blanket stitch to be "wonky"—another one of those technical terms. The problem with a high-end computerized sewing machine is it doesn't do wonky terribly well, so I had to help it along. If you look at the blanket stitching around the hand, you can see that it is perfect, with each stitch the same distance apart and the same width. To make the stitching on the heart look primitive, I kept my hand on the width knob and moved it back and forth while simultaneously kind of wobbling the fabric through the machine. The result is a very primitive look indeed.

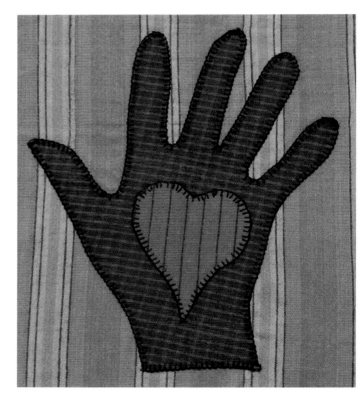

While sewing, manipulate the width of the blanket stitch to create a primitive look on the heart.

DECORATIVE STITCHES

Many machines come with dozens of beautiful decorative stitches that are appropriate for this type of appliqué. I suggest that you prepare some sample blocks—small ones will work fine—and give various stitches a try.

The heart samples shown below were first fused to a background square. Then, with a foundation paper underneath, I tried out some of the stitches with a variety of threads. I made notes on the foundation paper regarding the number of the stitch, the type of thread I used, and so on. This was a very useful exercise as I discovered some that I liked very much and some that, while pretty, did not seem substantial enough for the look I wanted.

Experiment with decorative stitches and a variety of threads.

NARROW ZIGZAG STITCH

So, what is the difference between a satin stitch and a
zigzag stitch? The difference is in the stitch length. A satin
stitch is a very short stitch that will completely cover
the fabric underneath. A zigzag stitch can be as short or
as long as you want it to be. It is not expected to cover
the underneath fabric, and is usually done with a thread
that will not show—invisible thread or one that matches
your appliqué. The satin stitch is most often used when
you want to see the thread—either to add some color or
to define an area. Of course both satin stitch and zigzag
stitches can be as wide or as narrow as you want them to
be. Consider whether they are to anchor your appliqué or
if you want them to add to the design.

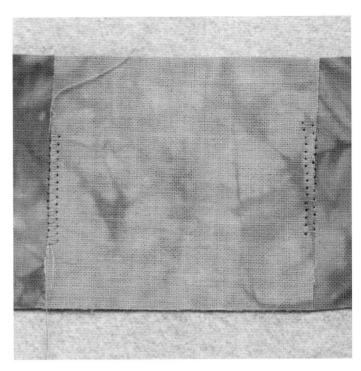

A zigzag stitch with cotton thread that blends with the appliqué is
shown on the left; a zigzag stitch with invisible thread is on the right.

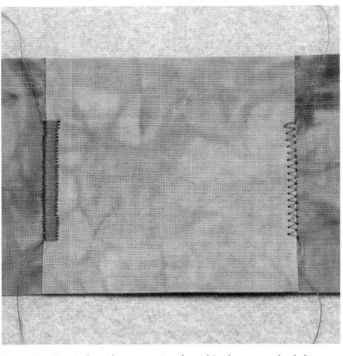

A satin stitch with contrasting thread is shown on the left;
a zigzag stitch with the same thread is on the right.

I often use a zigzag stitch in combination with fusible
appliqué for shapes that are very small or do not need
emphasis with stitching. I use invisible thread when I want
to stitch a fused shape but do not want the thread to show.
The stitch is similar to that used for invisible machine
appliqué, but a bit wider. Thread your machine with invisible nylon thread and a size 60/8 universal needle, fill
your bobbin with 50/3 medium gray thread, and set your
machine for a narrow zigzag stitch. Always test for stitch
length and tension on a scrap first.

This sample was stitched with invisible nylon thread, 60-weight cotton thread, and silk thread.

Side A: Pieced and quilted by the author

CRAZY HEARTS

When I teach my Machine Appliqué for the Terrified Quilter class, the motif we use to learn invisible and reverse appliqué is a heart. Over the years I've made hundreds of these hearts, and after every class I think, someday I'm going to make a quilt using this homely little heart. Well, I finally did. I decided to put 20 hearts on a quilt when my husband and I celebrated our twentieth wedding anniversary.

Techniques: Invisible Machine Appliqué, Reverse Appliqué, Reversible Quilt

Finished Quilt: 35½" x 42" ~ Finished Block: 6" x 6"

MATERIALS

All yardages are based on 42"-wide fabric.

2½ yards *total* of assorted white and off-white tone-on-tone prints for Crazy Quilt blocks, sashing, and binding (side A)

1 yard *total* of assorted blue, pink, and green tone-on-tone batiks for hearts, background blocks, and sashing (side A)

⅔ yard of black fabric for borders (side B)

⅔ yard of red striped fabric for sashing and binding (side B)

½ yard *total* of assorted black-on-white prints for blocks (side B)

½ yard *total* of assorted white-on-black prints for blocks (side B)

⅞ yard of 96"-wide fusible batting

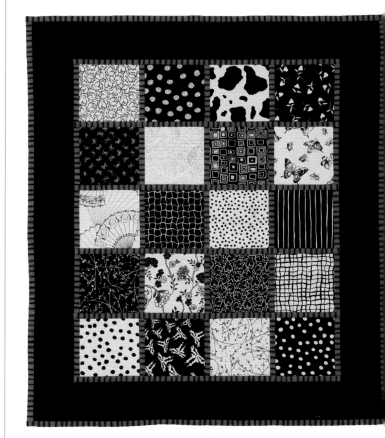

Side B

CUTTING

From the batting, cut:

20 squares, 7" x 7"

18 rectangles, 5" x 7"

4 squares, 5" x 5"

From the assorted blue, pink, and green tone-on-tone batiks, cut:

10 squares, 7" x 7"

10 squares, 5" x 5"

3 strips, 1¾" x 42"

From the assorted black-on-white prints, cut:

10 squares, 7" x 7"

From the assorted white-on-black prints, cut:

10 squares, 7" x 7"

From the assorted white and off-white tone-on-tone prints, cut:

7 strips*, 1¾" x 42"

18 pieces, 1¾" x 4½"

From the red striped fabric, cut:

10 strips, 1⅛" x 42"

From the black border fabric, cut:

4 strips, 5" x 42"; cut into 18 rectangles, 5" x 7", and 4 squares, 5" x 5"

18 pieces, 1⅛" x 4½"

If you are using scraps, you will need 4 strips at least 30" long, and 15 strips at least 7" long.

MAKING THE BLOCKS

I have always loved Crazy quilting. I've never done it with embroidery added; for me it's enough just to see all those leftover bits put to some use. But, who in their right mind wants to appliqué anything with all those seam allowances? For that reason, this is the perfect place to use reverse appliqué. When you see a Crazy quilted heart, it is underneath the batik background fabric that is, of course, seamless. Conversely, when you see a batik heart, it is appliquéd onto the Crazy quilting. In neither case did I have to worry about turning under those bulky seam allowances created by the Crazy quilting.

1. Referring to "Crazy Quilting" on page 35, construct 10 blocks that are 7" x 7" and 10 blocks that are 5" x 5". Do not fuse them to the batting squares yet.

2. Referring to "Preparing the Appliqués" on page 18 and "Reverse Appliqué" on page 20, appliqué 10 blocks with batik hearts (block A) and 10 blocks with hearts reverse appliquéd (block B). Use the heart pattern on page 37.

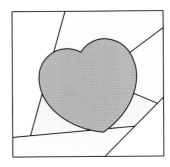

Block A.
Make 10 using 7" crazy quilt background and appliquéd heart.

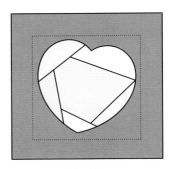

Block B.
Make 10 using 5" crazy quilt square underneath and reverse-appliqué the heart.

3. On a design wall, arrange the blocks in a manner that pleases you, alternating blocks A and B.

4. Arrange your black-and-white 7" squares on the design wall, directly on top of the appliquéd squares. Refer to the photo on page 33 as needed.

5. Working on one block at a time, place a black-and-white square face down on your ironing board, cover with a 7" square of fusible batting, and place either an A or B block on top, face up. Following the manufacturer's instructions, fuse the three layers together.

6. Quilt as desired. I quilted in the ditch around the hearts and on some of the stitching lines. Trim the blocks to 6½" x 6½".

7. Repeat steps 5 and 6 for all 20 blocks, making sure you return them to the correct position on your design wall.

CRAZY QUILTING

My version of Crazy quilting does not employ a foundation fabric; I just join pieces until I have the size I want. Usually I make the blocks reversible, so as soon as a block is the size I want, I fuse it to a batting square to stabilize it. I suggest creating a clear, see-through template or a window template the size of your finished block. You can use it to view your block to make sure it is big enough and decide how best to trim it.

1. Choose two fabric scraps and sew them with right sides together, using a ¼" seam. I usually start with one piece that has four nonparallel sides. I think of it as the center of the block, even though it might not end up right in the center. Press the seam away from the center piece, and trim the two sides straight. Subsequent pieces will be sewn to those two sides, so they should not be uneven.

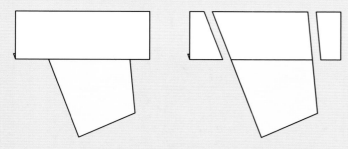

2. Stitch a third piece to whichever side you choose, press the seam toward the new piece, and trim so that the sides are straight.

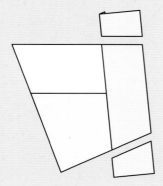

3. Continue in this manner, checking each new piece for length, pleasing color, and value before sewing into place.

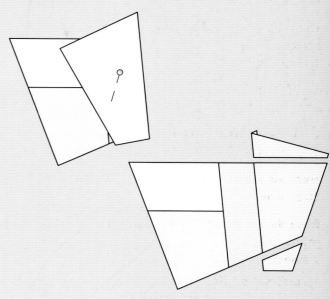

4. When you have the block approximately the size you need, check with a see-through template or window template to make sure it's big enough, and then trim to the size needed for your project. Be extremely careful when handling the blocks as they have bias edges all over.

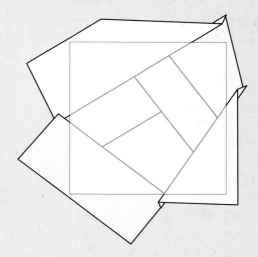

5. Add appliqué or embroidery to the block as desired. Layer the Crazy-pieced square, a square of fusible batting, and a backing square, and then fuse together and quilt as desired.

QUILT-TOP ASSEMBLY

Referring to "Basic Sashing" on page 100, sew the blocks together in rows, using the 1¾" white print strips and the 1⅛" red stripe strips. Sew the rows together with sashing.

ADDING THE BORDERS

When I made the blocks for the border, I joined them to the horizontal rows of hearts. As a result, I had to piece squares of the "inner-border" fabric when I sewed the rows together. I've simplified the construction and written the instructions so that the sashing that creates the inner border does not have to be pieced except along the top and bottom of the quilt.

1. Piece 18 Crazy Quilt blocks that are 5" x 7" and 4 blocks that are 5" x 5".

2. Working on one block at a time, place a black 5" x 7" rectangle face down on your ironing board, cover with a 5" x 7" piece of fusible batting, and place a 5" x 7" Crazy Quilt block on top, face up. Following the manufacturer's instructions, fuse the three layers together. Repeat with the black 5" x 5" squares, 5" x 5" batting squares, and the four 5" x 5" Crazy Quilt blocks.

3. Quilt as desired. I quilted in the ditch on some of the stitching lines. Trim the blocks to 4½" x 6½", and the four corner blocks to 4½" x 4½".

4. Referring to "Basic Sashing" on page 100, sew five of the 4½" x 6½" blocks together along the short edge using the 1¾" x 4½" white print sashing pieces (for the Crazy heart side) and the 1⅛" x 4½" black sashing pieces (for the red-and-black side) to make a side border. Repeat to make a second side border. In the same way, join four of the 4½" x 6½" blocks together with a 4½" x 4½" block at each end for the top border. Repeat for the bottom border.

5. Referring to "Reversible Borders with a Contrasting Inner Border" on page 103, join the side borders to the quilt with blue batik sashing strips on side A and red sashing strips on side B.

6. Referring to "Reversible Borders with a Contrasting Inner Border" on page 103, sew a border-fabric rectangle to each end of the sashing strips for the top and bottom. Make two for side A and two for side B. Join the borders to the quilt with the blue batik and white sashing strips on side A and red and black sashing strips on side B.

7. Referring to "Reversible Binding" on page 108, bind your quilt.

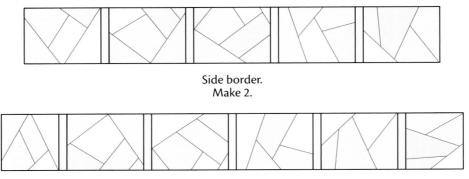

Side border.
Make 2.

Top/bottom border.
Make 2.

Heart

Appliquéd and quilted by the author; additional quilting by Coreen Zerr

XS AND OS

With the name Sharon, how could I write a book about machine appliqué and not include a Rose of Sharon–style quilt? I love the old ones and for inspiration I've kept a pile of photos of those I've seen in shows around the world. But, to keep the number of pattern pieces under control, I decided to make mine with only two main pattern pieces—the leaf is one, and the blossom in multiple sizes is the other. With just these two pattern pieces you can still make many different blocks.

TECHNIQUE: Invisible Machine Appliqué, Reversible Quilt

Finished Quilt: 46½" x 46½" ~ Finished Block: 12" x 12"

MATERIALS

All yardages are based on 42"-wide fabric.

1¼ yards of background fabric for blocks

1 yard *total* of assorted pink fabrics for blossoms

1 yard of batik for sashing and border

⅝ yard *total* of assorted green fabrics for leaves

½ yard of fabric for conventional binding OR

⅓ yard of fabric for reversible binding on front

¼ yard of fabric for reversible binding on back

2⅛ yards of fabric for backing

1⅛ yards of batting (based on 96"-wide batting)

CUTTING

From the background fabric, cut:
9 squares, 13" x 13"

From the assorted green fabrics, cut:
1"-wide straight-grain strips to total a length of 70"
1"-wide bias strips to total a length of 48"

From the batting, cut:
9 squares, 13" x 13"
6 pieces, 2" x 12"
2 strips, 2" x 40"
2 strips, 3¼" x 40"
2 strips, 3¼" x 46"

From the fabric for backing, cut:
9 squares, 13" x 13"
2 strips, 2½" x 42"; crosscut into 6 pieces, 2½" x 12½"
2 strips, 2½" x 40½"
5 strips, 3½" x 42"

From the batik, cut:
2 strips, 2½" x 42"; crosscut into 6 pieces, 2½" x 12½"
2 strips, 2½" x 40½"
5 strips, 3½" x 42"

MAKING THE BLOCKS

1. Referring to "Preparing the Appliqués" on page 18, trace and cut 140 F and 80 G leaf freezer-paper templates using the patterns on page 45.

2. Using as many different green fabrics as you wish, prepare the leaves for each block, making note of how many of each to make. Using the 1"-wide strips for stems, refer to "Making Stems" on page 42. Keep the straight grain and bias strips separate.

3. Trace and cut freezer-paper templates using the flower blossom patterns on page 45. You will need 6 A blossoms, 40 B blossoms, 6 C blossoms, 40 D blossoms, and 8 E blossoms.

4. Using as many different pink fabrics as you wish, prepare the blossoms for each block.

5. Make a full-size placement diagram for block 1. Draw a 12" x 12" square on paper and divide it in half vertically, horizontally, and diagonally. Draw a circle of 5"

radius and another one of 5⅛" radius. Trace a blossom E in each corner, placing the center of the blossom at the point where the diagonal line crosses the circles.

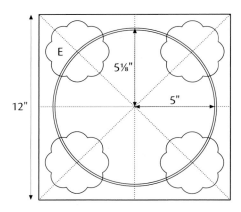

6. Put the block placement diagram on a light box. Fold one of the background squares in half horizontally and vertically; pinch the folds at the center to mark the center of the background. Match the center of your background fabric to the center of the placement diagram and position the appliqué pieces in the order they are to be stitched. For block 1, you will need 16 F leaves, 4 G leaves, 4 B blossoms, 4 D blossoms, 4 E blossoms, and four 5" prepared bias strips for stems.

7. Appliqué the stems first, then the G leaves, followed by the E blossoms, and then D and B. Finally stitch the F leaves. Remove the freezer paper as you go. Repeat to make two of block 1.

Block 1.
Make 2.

8. Make a full-size placement diagram for block 2. Draw a 12" x 12" square on paper and divide it in half vertically, horizontally, and diagonally. Draw a circle with a 1" radius in the center. Trace a D flower blossom so that the petal is 1" from the corners along the four diagonals.

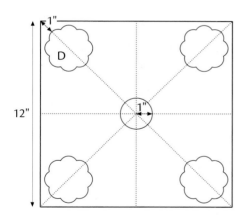

9. With the block placement diagram on a light box, position four 4½" straight-grain stems on the background square so that their ends touch the circle and they extend along the diagonals. Appliqué the stems. Position and appliqué 24 F leaves, four D blossoms, and then four B blossoms as shown. Repeat to make four of block 2.

Block 2.
Make 4.

10. Make a full-size placement diagram for block 3. Draw a 12" x 12" square on paper and divide it in half vertically, horizontally, and diagonally. Draw a circle with a 2⅝" radius in the center.

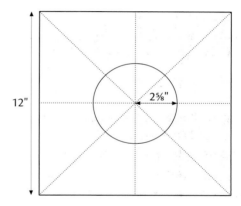

11. With the block placement guide on a light box, position eight D blossoms and 24 G leaves on the background fabric, using the circle and lines as guidance.

12. Remove the blossoms so that you can baste each group of three G leaves in position as shown. Appliqué only the top leaf in each group of three.

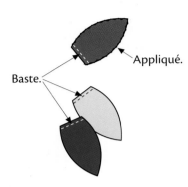

Appliqué.

Baste.

13. Arrange and appliqué one D blossom and then a B blossom on top of the leaves, removing freezer paper as you go. Working counterclockwise, appliqué the next pair of leaves. Leave the two basted leaves on the right unsewn until the end, as all the blossoms must be appliquéd before they can be stitched down.

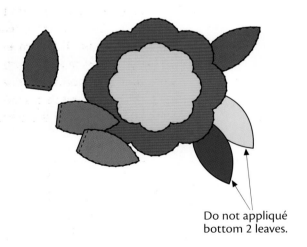

Do not appliqué bottom 2 leaves.

MAKING STEMS

If the stem is straight, it is not necessary to use bias strips. However, for curved stems you'll want to use bias strips. The steps are the same for both.

1. Cut as many 1"-wide strips as you need, either on the bias or on the straight grain.

2. Fold the strip in half lengthwise, wrong sides together, and press.

3. With a ⅛" seam allowance, sew the raw edges together.

4. Fold the strip in half lengthwise again, centering the raw edges in the middle, and press.

5. Cut strips into the lengths needed and position them on the background fabric. Stitch in place, referring to "Stitching the Appliqué" on page 19. The raw edges on the ends will be covered by flower petals, so they do not need to be turned under or stitched.

14. Continue appliquéing around the circle. When you reach the final set of blossoms, fold the loose leaves out of the way to appliqué the blossoms. Once they are stitched in place, you can then stitch the two remaining leaves.

15. Make two of block 3.

Block 3.
Make 2.

16. Make a full-sized placement diagram for block 4. Draw a 12" square on paper and draw a horizontal and vertical line through the center. Draw a circle with a radius of 4". Measure in from each corner 2½" and place a tiny mark along the top and bottom edges of the block. Draw an X through the center connecting the points. Trace the C blossom template six times, aligning an outer petal edge along the circle and placing the center point on a diagonal line.

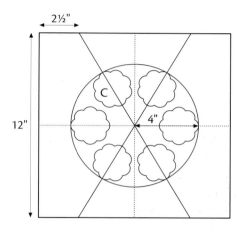

17. With the block placement guide on a light box, position 12 F leaves and 24 G leaves along the horizontal and diagonal lines. Position them in sets of three with the G leaves underneath, and appliqué. The F leaves should be 1½" away from the C blossom and ½" from the outer edge of the block along the horizontal line. Position and appliqué six C blossoms and then six A blossoms. You need only one of block 4 for the center of the quilt.

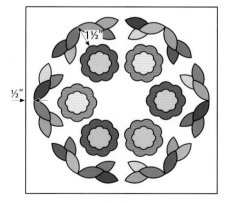

Block 4.
Make 1.

QUILTING THE BLOCKS

1. Layer each block with a 13" square of batting and a 13" square of backing. Place the backing wrong side up, add the batting, and then add the block, right side up. Hobbs Fusible Batting is a good choice here. Fuse or pin the layers together.

2. Quilt as desired and trim each block to 12½" x 12½".

QUILT ASSEMBLY

1. Arrange the blocks in three rows of three blocks each.

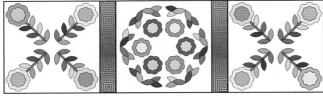

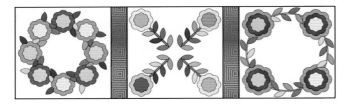

2. Refer to "Wide Sashing" on page 101. Using the 2½"-wide sashing and backing pieces and the 2"-wide batting pieces, sew the blocks into rows. Quilt the sashing as you go.

3. Join the rows with wide sashing and do the quilting as you go.

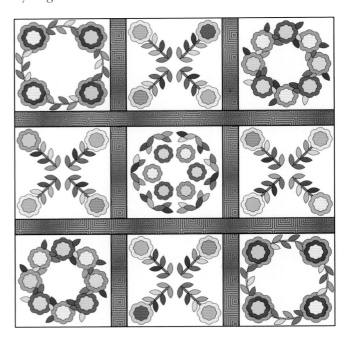

4. Referring to "Terre's Borders" on page 104, add the borders to the quilt using the 3½"-wide strips of batik and backing fabric and the 3¼" strips of batting.

FINISHING THE QUILT

As the quilting is already finished, all that's left to do is add binding and a hanging sleeve to your quilt. Refer to "Basic Binding" on page 107 and "Hanging Sleeves" on page 106.

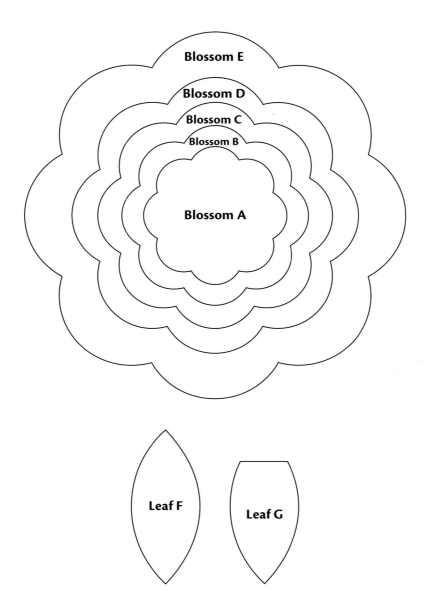

Blossom E

Blossom D

Blossom C

Blossom B

Blossom A

Leaf F

Leaf G

Pieced and quilted by the author

DOUBLE WEDDING RING

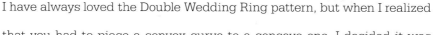
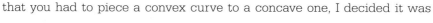

I have always loved the Double Wedding Ring pattern, but when I realized that you had to piece a convex curve to a concave one, I decided it was not on the top of my "to do" list. However, when I started thinking about it, I realized that it was a perfect candidate for machine appliqué. With some practice and a little help from Electric Quilt, I was able to create the template pieces to make my first Double Wedding Ring quilt. I was more than a little pleased with how much easier it was while still giving me the wonderful traditional look I wanted. (Electric Quilt is a wonderful computer program for designing quilts; see "Resources" on page 110.)

TECHNIQUE: Invisible Machine Appliqué

Finished Quilt: 40½" x 40½"

MATERIALS

All yardages are based on 42"-wide fabric.

2 yards of black fabric for blocks, corner triangles, and binding

1 yard *total* of assorted black-and-white prints for arcs

½ yard of white fabric for center half-square triangles

2½ yards of fabric for backing*

44" x 44" piece of batting

8½" x 11" piece of template plastic

*If your backing fabric is at least 42" wide, 1⅓ yards will be enough.

CUTTING

From the black fabric, cut:

4 squares, 8½" x 8½"

8 rectangles, 8½" x 12½"

2 squares, 13" x 13"; cut each square once diagonally to yield 4 triangles

32 squares, 2½" x 2½"

5 strips, 2½" x 40"

From the white fabric, cut:

2 squares, 13" x 13"; cut each square once diagonally to yield 4 triangles

PREPARING THE ARCS

Trace patterns A and B on page 51 onto template plastic using a permanent marker. (If you wish to make a pieced arc, see page 53.) Cut out the shapes. Transfer the place-ment-guide markings to template B with the permanent marker. If you prefer, see "Resources" on page 110 to purchase a set of acrylic templates like those shown.

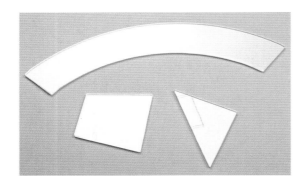

1. Referring to "Preparing the Appliqués" on page 18, cut 24 freezer-paper templates using template A.

2. Iron the freezer-paper templates to the wrong side of the black-and-white fabrics. Cut around each template, leaving between 1/8" and 1/4" seam allowance on the curved sides and 1/2" on the ends.

3. Apply rubber cement to the curved edges of the arc pieces and turn seam allowances under. It is not necessary to glue or turn under the ends of the arcs; they will be covered by the corner triangles. Repeat for all 24 arcs.

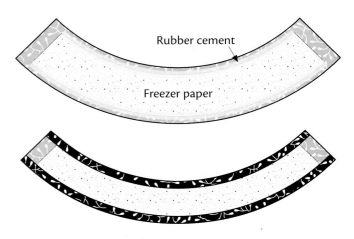

MAKING THE BACKGROUND BLOCKS

1. Sew a large white triangle to a large black triangle, being careful not to stretch the bias edges; press seams toward the black fabric. Trim to 12½" x 12½". Repeat with the remaining triangles to make four background blocks.

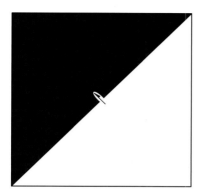

Make 4.

2. Arrange the blocks on your design wall so that the four white triangles are toward the center.

APPLIQUÉING THE BLOCKS

1. Fold one 12½" background block in half vertically and finger-press to mark the center. Fold one arc in half to find its center and finger-press. Place the arc on the background square, matching fold lines as shown. Use template B in the corners to help position the arc, turning it over as needed for the opposite corners. The ends of the arc should be within the placement lines on your template—or close. Remember, we are not doing brain surgery, so if it's not exact your quilt will still be beautiful. Tape in place.

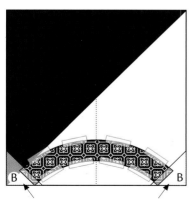

The placement guide is on top of the arc for positioning.

2. Referring to "Stitching the Appliqué" on page 19, stitch the arc in place and remove the freezer paper.

3. Repeat for the remaining arcs, removing freezer paper as you go. The arcs may overlap a bit at the corners; this is fine. Make four center blocks with four arcs on each.

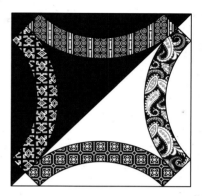

Make 4.

4. Using the 8½" x 12½" black rectangles, make eight rectangular blocks with one arc each.

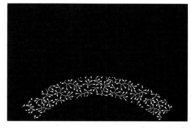

Make 8.

ADDING THE CORNER TRIANGLES

1. Place a 2½" black square on the corner of a 12½" block with right sides together. Draw a diagonal line from corner to corner and sew on the line.

2. Trim excess fabric, leaving a ¼" seam allowance. Repeat for all four corners and all four blocks. Press the seams toward the corner in two of the blocks and toward the center in the other two so that when the blocks are sewn together the seam allowances will go in alternate directions.

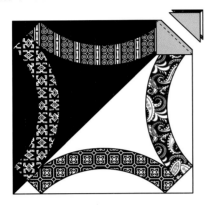

Make 4.

3. Repeat the process to sew squares to two corners of each rectangular block. As each block is finished, place it on your design wall.

QUILT-TOP ASSEMBLY

1. Sew the blocks and 8½" black squares together in rows, making sure the arcs on each block are positioned as shown. Insert a pin at the point where the arc meets the triangle to align it with the corresponding point of the block next to it. Press seams in alternate directions from row to row.

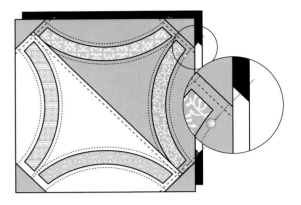

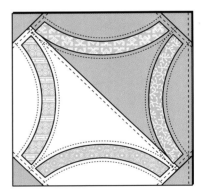

2. Sew the rows together, pressing seams in one direction.

FINISHING THE QUILT

1. Referring to "Layering, Basting, and Quilting" on page 105, layer the batting, backing, and quilt top together. Baste with pins, or fuse if you're using fusible batting.

2. Quilt as desired.

3. Referring to "Hanging Sleeves" on page 106, add a hanging sleeve.

4. Referring to "Basic Binding" on page 107, bind the edges of the quilt with the black strips.

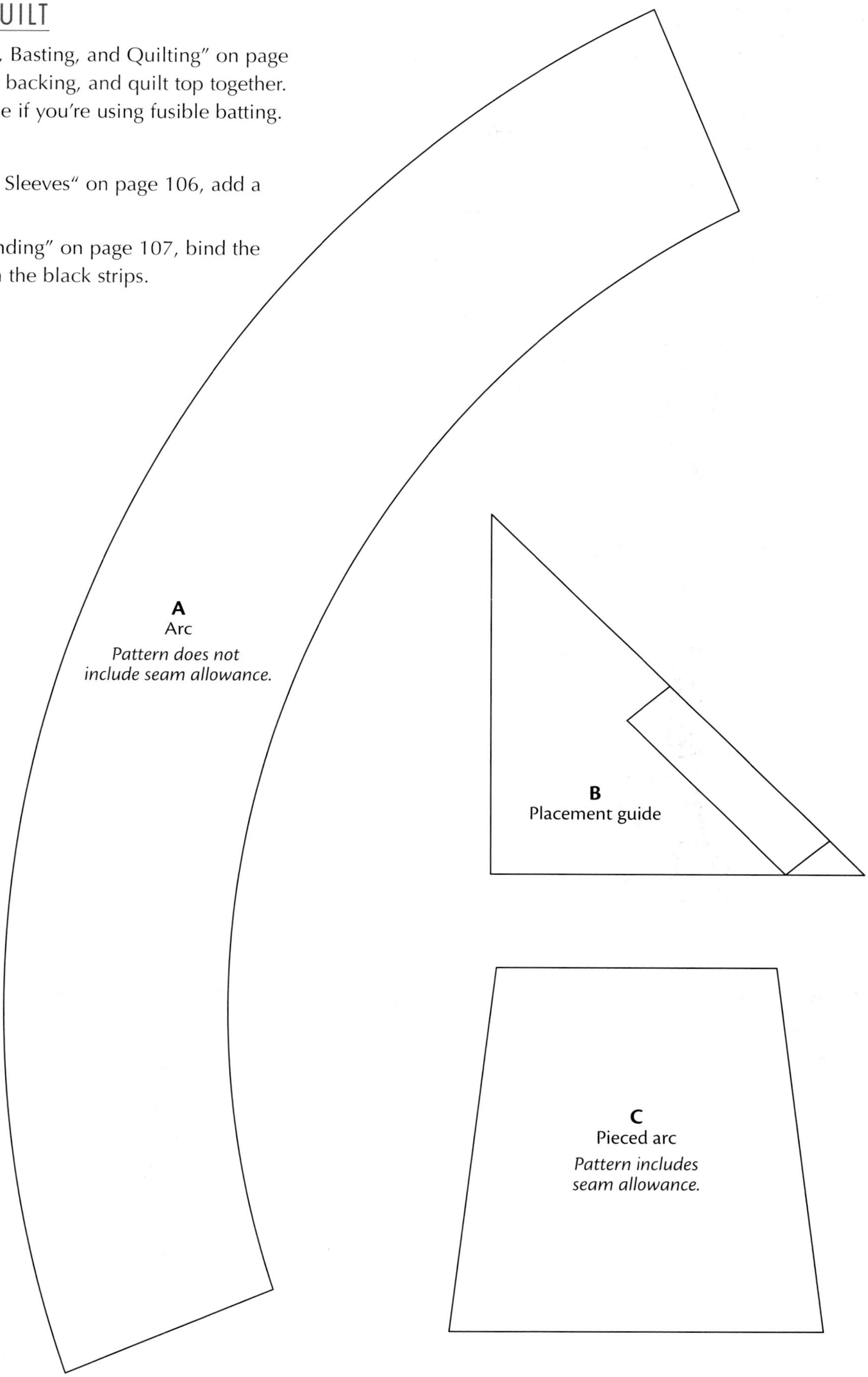

A
Arc
*Pattern does not
include seam allowance.*

B
Placement guide

C
Pieced arc
*Pattern includes
seam allowance.*

Pieced and quilted by the author

PIECED ARCS

1. To make a quilt with pieced arcs, trace patterns A, B, and C on page 51 onto template plastic and cut out.

2. Cut six pieces for each arc. Each piece can be cut from a different fabric if you wish. When using scraps, make sure the grain line is parallel to, or at right angles to, the top of the template. To cut multiple pieces from one fabric, cut a 2½" strip from the chosen fabric and use the template to cut out as many shapes from that fabric as you want.

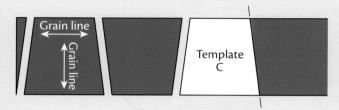

3. With a ¼" seam, sew six pieces together with the wide end matching the next wide end. Press seams open.

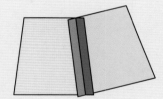

4. Follow step 1 of "Preparing the Arcs" on page 48 to make freezer-paper templates. Fold a freezer-paper arc in half to find the center. Place it on the wrong side of a pieced arc, matching the fold with the center seam of the pieced arc. Press and trim, leaving a ¼" seam allowance on the curved sides. Do not trim anything off the ends.

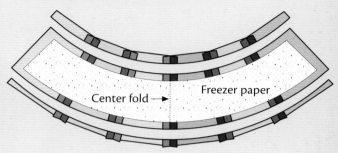

5. Using the pieced arcs, continue with step 3 of "Preparing the Arcs" and follow the rest of the instructions for making the quilt.

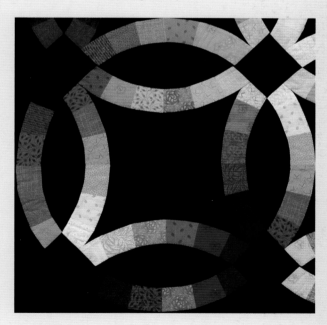

Designed and pieced by Gail MacRae;
quilted by the author

GAIL'S GARDEN

My daughter Gail came to visit one summer while I was working on my first stained-glass quilt. Being a quilter, she asked if I would show her how to do it, which of course I was happy to do. Gail finished the little purple flower I had given her and when she got home she designed and made two more flower blocks, putting them all together to make this charming wall hanging. When I was collecting quilts for this book I asked her if she would let me use it. She agreed, on one condition—that I quilt it.

Finished Quilt: 14" x 38¾" ~ Finished Block: 7½" x 9¾"

MATERIALS

All yardages are based on 42"-wide fabric.

¾ yard of blue batik for sashing, borders, and binding*

⅜ yard of light blue fabric for blocks

⅓ yard of black fabric for blocks

Assorted scraps of red, yellow, purple, and green fabric for flowers and leaves

18" x 42" piece of backing fabric

18" x 42" piece of batting

If your fabric is a stripe, similar to that used in the photo, and you want all the stripes to run vertically, purchase 1 yard of fabric.

CUTTING

From the black fabric, cut:
3 rectangles, 8½" x 11"

From the blue batik, cut:
2 strips, 2" x 8"
2 strips, 3½" x 14"
2 strips, 3½" x 32¾"
3 strips, 2½" x 42"

MAKING THE BLOCKS

1. Referring to "Preparing the Appliqués" on page 18, trace the three flower patterns on pages 56–60 onto the dull side of three 8½" x 11" pieces of freezer paper.

2. Cut out the designs, cutting on every drawn line, and then iron one freezer-paper pattern to the wrong side of each 8½" x 11" piece of black fabric.

3. Referring to "Reverse Appliqué" on page 20, cut away all the open areas (flower, leaves, and sky), leaving between ⅛" and ¼" for seam allowance. Glue and turn the seam allowances under.

4. Position a sky, petal, or leaf fabric underneath the corresponding opening and tape it to keep it from shifting. (It doesn't matter where you begin.) Referring to "Stitching the Appliqué" on page 19, stitch in place. Turn over and trim the excess fabric. Note that the sky pieces can be sewn in many small sections, or sewn by placing one large piece of blue fabric behind the black piece. After stitching, trim away excess fabric.

5. Continue adding all petal, leaf, and sky fabrics until the flower block is complete. When all stitching is complete, remove the freezer paper. Trim each block to 8" x 10¼".

QUILT-TOP ASSEMBLY

1. Sew a 2" x 8" sashing strip between the rose block and the daffodil block, and sew the remaining 2" x 8" strip between the daffodil block and the orchid block. Press seams toward the sashing strips.

2. Referring to "Basic Borders" on page 102, sew the 3½" x 32¾" side borders onto the quilt. Press the seams toward the border.

3. Sew the 3½" x 14" top and bottom borders to the quilt. Press seams toward the border.

FINISHING THE QUILT

1. Referring to "Layering, Basting, and Quilting" on page 105, layer the batting, backing, and quilt top together. Baste with pins, or fuse if you're using fusible batting.

2. Quilt as desired.

3. Referring to "Hanging Sleeves" on page 106, add a hanging sleeve.

4. Referring to "Basic Binding" on page 107, bind the edges of the quilt.

Each section could be created as a small wall hanging if you wish.

Rose

Daffodil

Orchid

BEST FRIENDS

My good friend Judie Hansen is a wonderful artist and one of her special-ties is cartooning. I love finding an envelope in my mailbox with her return address on it, because I know that what's inside will make me laugh. This delightful quilt was originally a birthday card from Judie to me. I then turned it into a wall hanging, which I gave her for her birthday. The quilt shown has our countries' flags on our sweatshirts, but feel free to have fun. Personalize it with whatever fabric motifs suit you—your guild logo, your high school emblem, whatever will make it truly your own.

TECHNIQUE: Fusible Appliqué

Finished Quilt: 15½" x 17½"

MATERIALS

All yardages are based on 42"-wide fabric.

⅜ yard of red fabric for border and binding

⅛ yard of red-and-white checked fabric for faux piping

10½" x 12½" piece of fabric for background

18" x 20" piece of fabric for backing

18" x 20" piece of batting

Assorted scraps for clothing, hair, and skin

Designed by Judie Hansen; pieced and quilted by the author

CUTTING

From the red-and-white checked fabric, cut:

2 pieces, 1" x 10½"

2 pieces, 1" x 12½"

From the red fabric, cut:

2 rectangles, 3" x 10½"

2 rectangles, 3" x 17½"

2 strips, 2½" x 42"

APPLIQUÉING THE CENTER

1. Referring to "Working with Fusible Web" on page 21, prepare the pattern pieces for "Judie" and "Sharon" on pages 64 and 65.

2. Referring to the placement guide on page 65, place the appliqué pieces in position on the 10½" x 12½" piece of background fabric. When you are certain you have them where you want them, fuse in place.

3. Thread your machine with invisible nylon thread and a size 60/8 universal needle, fill your bobbin with 50/3 medium gray thread, and set your machine for a narrow zigzag stitch. Test for stitch length and tension on a scrap.

4. Stitch around the edges of all the appliqué pieces.

QUILT-TOP ASSEMBLY

1. Referring to "Faux Piping" on page 104, stitch the red-and-white check strips to the top and bottom of the quilt, and then to the sides.

2. Sew the 3" x 10½" border pieces to the top and bottom of the quilt, and press seams toward the border. Sew the 3" x 17½" border pieces to the sides of the quilt, and press seams toward the border.

FINISHING THE QUILT

1. Referring to "Layering, Basting, and Quilting" on page 105, layer the batting, backing, and quilt top together. Baste with pins, or fuse if you're using fusible batting.

2. Thread your machine with black cotton thread. Use your darning foot to free-motion quilt around all the appliqué pieces; or use a walking foot as I did, and simply pivot like crazy. Add other definition lines as shown in the placement diagram. Stitching the facial features is optional. I used a fine-point permanent pen to draw the mouth and eyes, but I stitched the nose and eyebrows.

3. Referring to "Hanging Sleeves" on page 106, add a hanging sleeve.

4. Referring to "Basic Binding" on page 107, bind the edges of the quilt with the red strips.

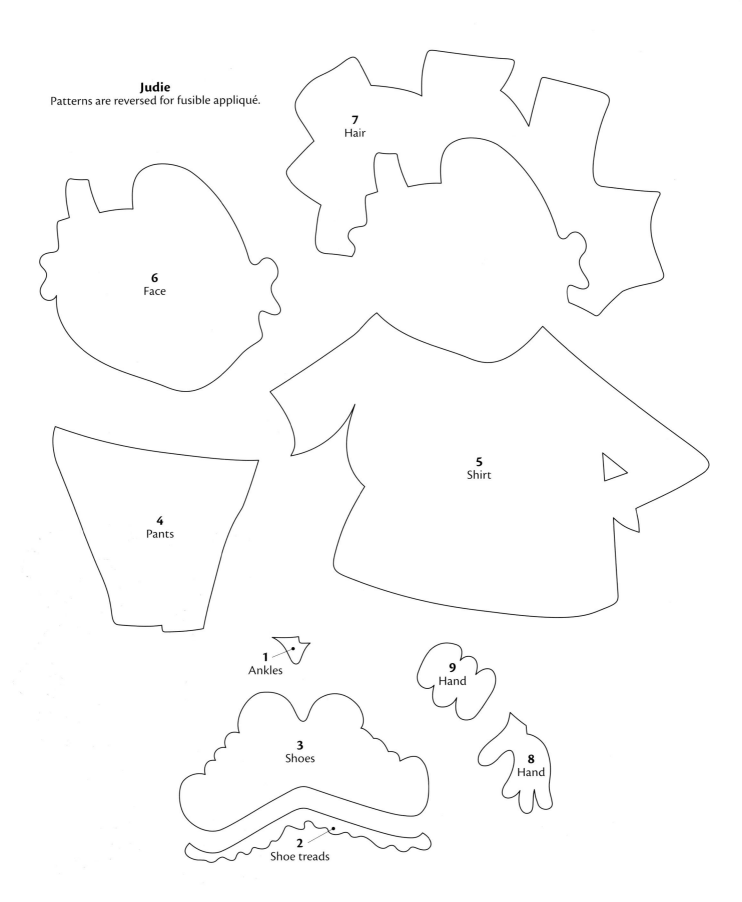

Judie
Patterns are reversed for fusible appliqué.

7
Hair

6
Face

5
Shirt

4
Pants

1
Ankles

3
Shoes

2
Shoe treads

9
Hand

8
Hand

6
Hair

Sharon
Patterns are reversed for fusible appliqué.

8
Hand

3
Pants

5
Face

7
Hand

4
Shirt

1
Feet

2
Shoes

Placement guide

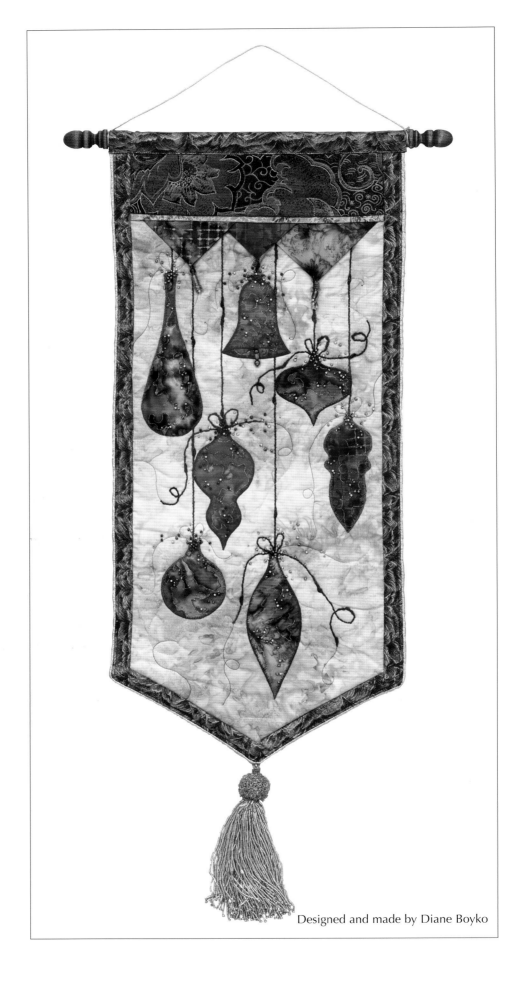

Designed and made by Diane Boyko

DECK THE HALLS

For my local quilt guild's Christmas party we were asked to bring appropriate quilts to decorate the hall. One wall hanging very quickly attracted a crowd. It was my friend Diane Boyko's delightful little quilt, and we all just loved it. Diane is a wonderfully creative quilter and I always look forward to her appearances at show-and-tell. In keeping with the Christmas spirit, she very generously agreed to share her beautiful, original design with us.

TECHNIQUE: Fusible Appliqué

Finished Quilt: 13" x 29"

MATERIALS

All yardages are based on 42"-wide fabric.

½ yard of very light mauve batik for background

¼ yard *total* of assorted batiks for appliqués

¼ yard *total* of 3 different batiks for prairie points

¼ yard of green-and-gold print for outer borders and hanging tube

⅛ yard of purple-and-green print for top border

1" x 12" piece of gold-and-green print for faux piping

15" x 31" piece of fabric for backing

15" x 31" piece of fusible batting

2 yards of purchased gold lamé piping

Decorative threads for ornament hangers

13" hanging rod with removable finials

1 yard of gold cord for hanging

Beads for embellishment (optional)

Gold tassel (optional)

CUTTING

From the light mauve batik, cut:
1 piece, 12" x 25"

From the purple-and-green print, cut:
1 piece, 3¼" x 12"

From the batiks for prairie points, cut:
1 square, 4" x 4"
1 square, 4½" x 4½"
1 square, 6¾" x 6¾"

From the green-and-gold print, cut:
2 strips, 1¼" x 42"; crosscut each strip into 1 strip, 1¼" x 28", and 1 strip, 1¼" x 12"

PREPARING THE BACKGROUND

1. Fold the light mauve background fabric in half length-wise and finger-press the center. On the raw edges, measure 3" up from the bottom of the background fabric. Using a ruler and rotary cutter, cut off the corners from the raw edge to the center.

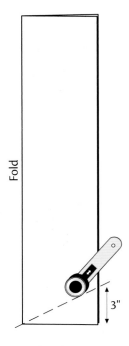

2. Cut decorative threads for the ornaments as follows. The lengths allow an extra 1". The threads will extend ½" above the seam line of the background (¼" beyond the background) and ½" will be covered by the ornament.

   Ornament 1: 3"

   Ornament 2: 15¾"

   Ornament 3: 10"

   Ornament 4: 3¼"

   Ornament 5: 16"

   Ornament 6: 7"

   Ornament 7: 10"

3. Referring to the placement diagram at right, measure from the left side of the background for each ornament string. Draw the position of each of the seven hanging

strings and ornaments lightly on the background fabric. Referring to "Couching" on page 74, couch the decorative hanging threads in place. Be sure to end each hanging thread ½" below the top of the ornament so that when you fuse it in place the ornament will cover the raw end of the thread. The top of each thread will be enclosed in the seam.

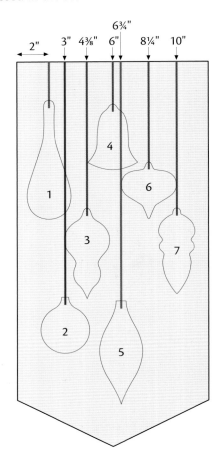

4. Using the three assorted batik squares, make prairie points by folding each one diagonally twice. Press lightly.

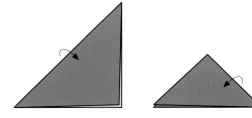

5. Place each prairie point as shown, nesting the two on the right inside the one to the left. Align the raw edges with the top edge of the background fabric, and make sure the point aligns with the couched hanging thread below. Baste in place.

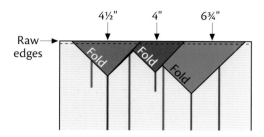

6. Fold the 1" x 12" gold-and-green faux piping strip in half lengthwise and press. Place on top of the prairie points, lining up the raw edges with the raw edge of the background fabric; baste in place.

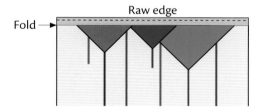

7. With right sides together, place the 3¼" x 12" purple-and-green border piece on top of the prairie points and faux piping. Sew in place with a ¼" seam. Press the seam toward the border.

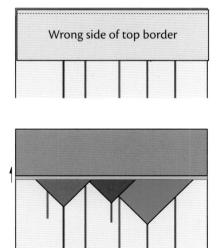

8. Sew a 1¼" x 12" green-and-gold border strip to the lower-right angled edge of the quilt. Press and trim even with the two adjoining sides. Repeat for the lower-left angled edge.

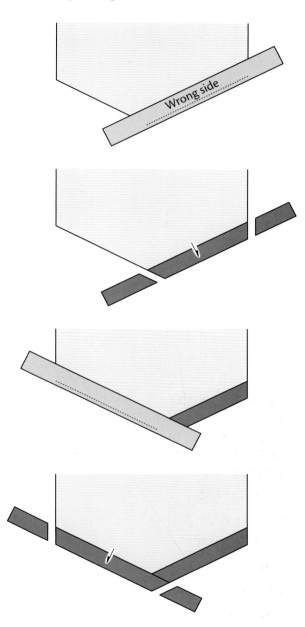

9. Sew the 1¼" x 28" green-and-gold strips to the sides. Press and trim.

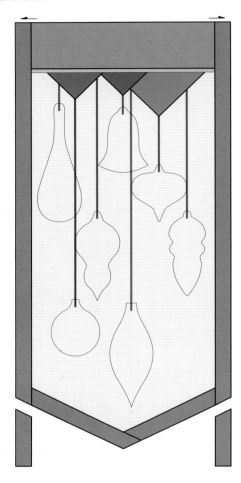

APPLIQUÉING THE ORNAMENTS

1. Refer to "Working with Fusible Web" on page 21. Use the patterns on pages 72 and 73 to prepare the seven ornaments. Arrange them on the placement lines drawn on the background, making sure to cover the ends of the hanging threads by ½". When you are pleased with the arrangement, fuse in place.

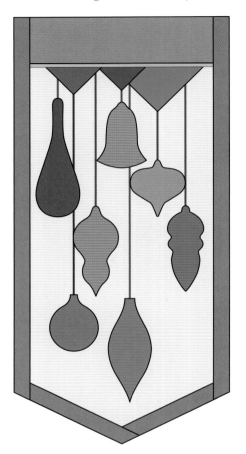

2. Referring to "The Satin Stitch" on page 22 or using a decorative stitch on your machine, stitch around each ornament. Diane stitched hers with a type of blanket stitch. Don't forget to use a foundation paper underneath. A shiny rayon thread would be a good choice for these shimmering ornaments.

LAYERING THE TOP

1. Cut a piece of backing fabric and a piece of fusible batting exactly the same size as your quilt top. Fuse the batting to the wrong side of the backing fabric following the manufacturer's instructions.

2. Line up the raw edge of the gold lamé piping with the raw edge of the wall hanging. Using a zipper foot on your machine, and a scant ¼" seam allowance, sew the piping to the outside edges, clipping the piping seam allowance at the corners. Do not add piping across the top.

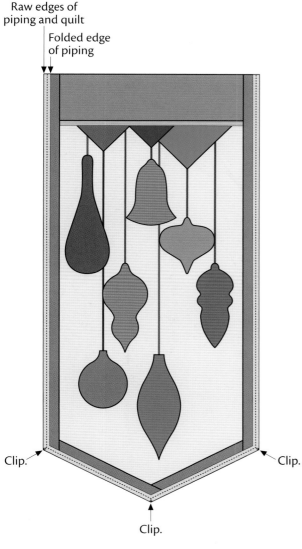

Raw edges of piping and quilt

Folded edge of piping

Clip.

Clip.

Clip.

3. With right sides together, pin the backing-and-batting piece to the top of the wall hanging, being careful to keep the piping inside the stitching line.

4. With the zipper foot still on your machine, stitch the sides and bottom of the wall hanging together, staying just inside the piping stitching line. Trim any excess batting from the seam allowance and turn the layers right side out. Press.

QUILTING AND FINISHING

1. Quilt as desired. Diane used a variegated thread for much of the quilting.

2. To add the ribbons and bows to the ornaments, refer to "Couching" on page 74. Diane used a beautiful, heavyweight multicolored thread that she stitched on with her couching foot and invisible thread. Leave long tails of thread at the beginning and ending of your stitching. After couching, use a needle with a large eye to pull the tails through to bury them in the batting.

3. Measure the circumference of your hanging rod. Cut a strip 15" long by that measurement plus about ¾" (½" for seams and ⅛" to ¼" for ease when inserting the rod); hem the short ends. Turn under ¼" on one long edge and press.

¼"

4. On the back of the quilt, align the raw edge of the hanging tube (not the turned-under edge) with the raw edge of the quilt, right sides together. Sew in place with a ¼" seam.

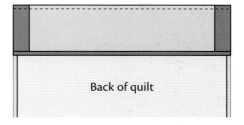

Back of quilt

5. Turn the folded edge to the front of the quilt. With gold thread in your machine, topstitch in place.

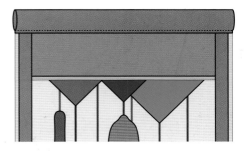

6. Embellish with beads, if desired, and add a gold hanging cord and a purchased tassel.

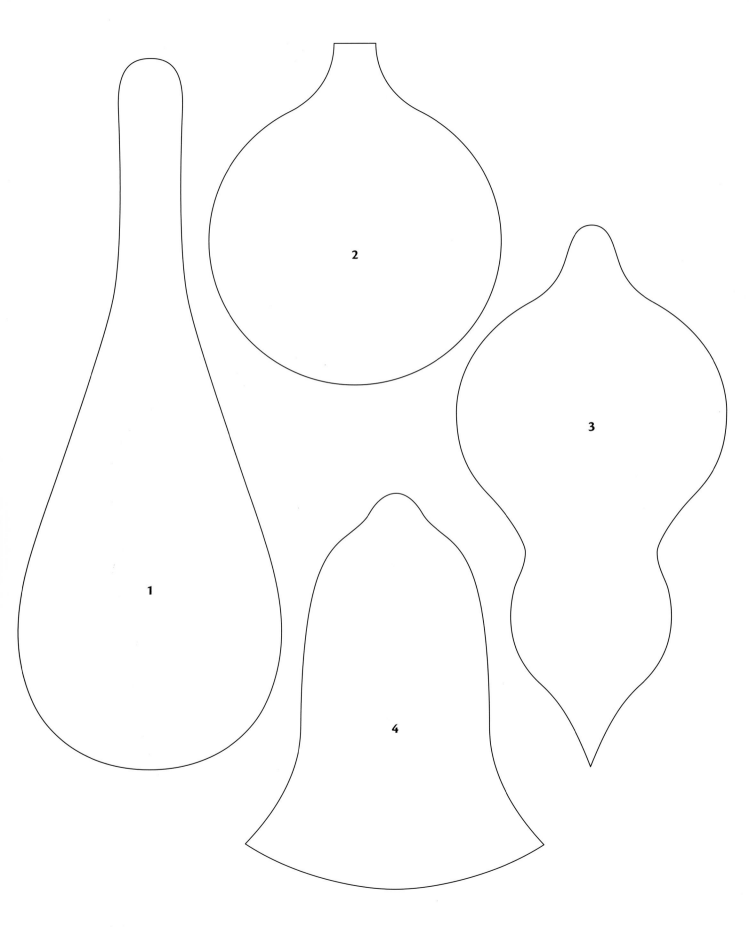

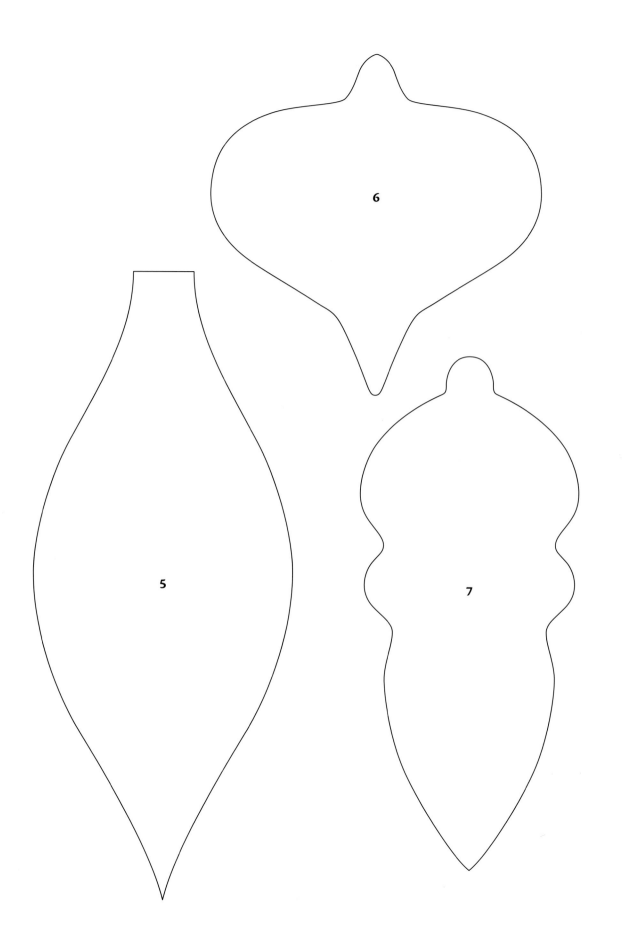

6

5

7

COUCHING

You will need to buy a special foot to successfully couch heavy threads onto your quilts, but it is worth the investment. With it you can add all sorts of wonderful embellishments that cannot be sewn with either the needle or the bobbin. The foot can also be used to add multiple strands at the same time, allowing you to blend different threads to create the perfect multicolored thread for your project.

The foot has a large hole in the top just in front of the oval-shaped hole for the needle. The heavy thread is fed through the hole from the top, then fed under the foot and pulled to the back. Choose a stitch that goes from side to side—it can be a plain zigzag or a decorative stitch. When beginning, anchor the thread with very tiny stitches, and then sew with the chosen stitch. Do some practice stitches with your couching thread and your needle thread to find the prettiest combination. Anchor the thread again when you reach the end of the couching. Sometimes you want to see only the couched threads; in that case, use an invisible thread in the needle.

Couching foot

This sample was couched with a fluffy white yarn to make the sheep look woolly.

To easily feed the thread from the spool, I threaded the spool onto the knee lift on my machine. If you don't have a knee lift or if you are using spools that won't fit on it, use a plastic straw with a rubber band wound around the end to hold the spool. Insert the open end under the front of the machine (the weight of the machine will keep it in place).

Multiple strands of decorative threads can be stitched at the same time. This allows you to create your own color scheme or special effect. Keeping the couching thread from getting tangled can sometimes be a problem, so I created a guide using a piece of cardboard and a hole punch. Count the number of threads you plan to use and put a hole for each one in the cardboard. Tape the cardboard to the front of your machine and thread each piece through a hole. With this system, I am able to handle three or four threads simultaneously.

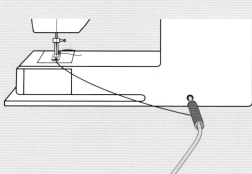

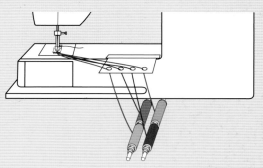

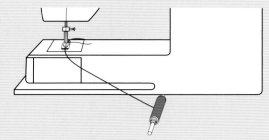

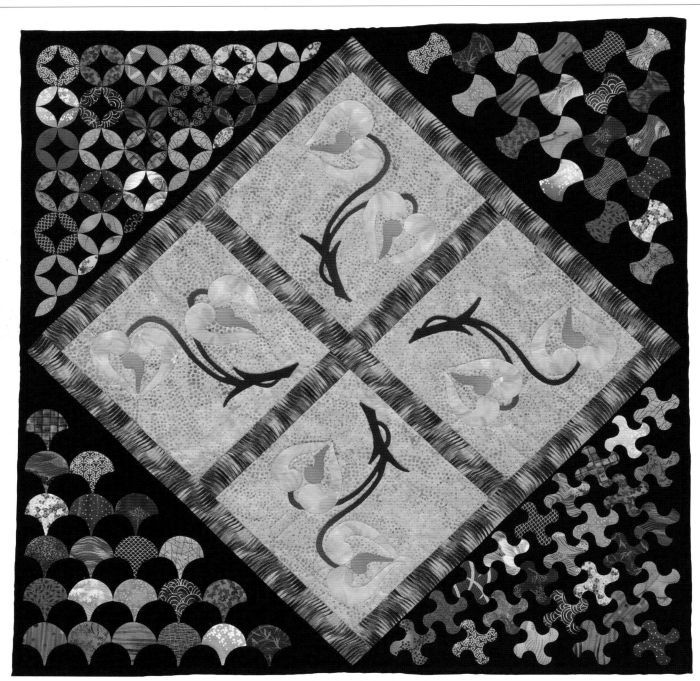

Designed and made by the author

SASHIKO REVISITED

My love affair with Japanese design continues, and while I was choosing patterns I decided that some of the beautiful Sashiko designs I had used in my book *Sensational Sashiko* would work equally well as appliqué patterns. So, the corner designs are (clockwise from the top left): Seven Treasures of Buddha, Counterweights, Plover, and Clamshell. I used two different methods to appliqué the Sashiko designs—I turned under the edges of the Clamshell and Counterweights designs, but when it came to Seven Treasures of Buddha and Plover, I decided that fusing was the better choice.

For the center motifs, I used a beautiful Japanese Family Crest from the Dover book *Japanese Design Motifs*. See "Resources" on page 110 for information.

TECHNIQUES: Invisible Machine Appliqué, Fusible Appliqué, Reversible Quilt

Finished Quilt: 38" x 38" ~ Finished Block: 11" x 11"

MATERIALS

All yardages are based on 42"-wide fabric.

2⅝ yards of navy blue fabric for corner backgrounds, backing, sashing for the back, and binding

⅞ yard of light blue batik for background squares

⅞ yard *total* of assorted blue prints for appliqués

⅜ yard of blue striped fabric for sashing

⅓ yard of light orange fabric for flowers

¼ yard of brown fabric for stems

⅛ yard of dark orange fabric for flowers

¾ yard of batting (based on 96"-wide batting)

8½" x 11" piece of template plastic

CUTTING

From the light blue batik, cut:

4 squares, 12" x 12"

From the navy blue fabric, cut:

4 squares, 12" x 12"

4 squares, 20" x 20"; cut each square once diagonally to yield 8 triangles (4 each for the front and back)

2 strips, 2" x 11½"

3 strips, 2" x 24"

2 strips, 2" x 27"

5 strips, 2½" x 40"

From the batting, cut:

4 squares, 12" x 12"

2 squares, 20" x 20"; cut each square once diagonally to yield 4 triangles

2 strips, 1½" x 11½"

3 strips, 1½" x 24"

2 strips, 1½" x 27"

From the blue striped fabric, cut:

2 strips, 2" x 11½"

3 strips, 2" x 24"

2 strips, 2" x 27"

Family Crest block

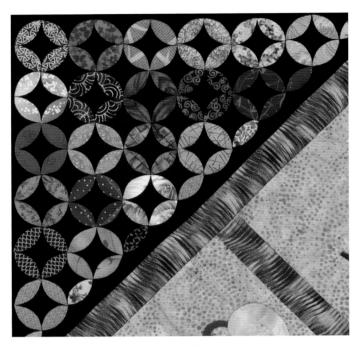

Seven Treasures of Buddha corner block

MAKING THE CENTER APPLIQUÉ BLOCKS

1. Referring to "Preparing the Appliqués" on page 18 and using the patterns on page 82, make freezer-paper templates and prepare the flowers and stem pieces for appliqué. Do not glue or turn under the stem ends marked with an X; they will be covered by flowers later.

2. Position the stem pieces on the 12" background square. Remove the larger stem piece. Tape the small stems in place and stitch, followed by the larger stem piece, and then the flowers. Make four.

Appliqué placement diagram

3. After stitching, turn the blocks over and cut away the excess background fabric, leaving ¼" seam allowance. Remove the freezer paper, but don't worry if you can't get all the paper out of the stem pieces.

MAKING THE CORNER APPLIQUÉ BLOCKS

1. On all of the corner triangle pieces, mark ¾" in from each of the short sides, and from these lines draw a 2½" grid on three of them. The fourth triangle does not need a grid on it. My favorite marker for drawing on dark fabrics is the Clover White Marking Pen, an iron-off marker that disappears with a little puff of steam from your iron.

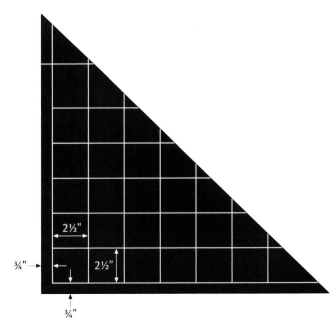

2. Using the patterns on page 83, make plastic templates for each design, making sure you keep both the positive and negative images. Sometimes it's better to work with the negative image; for instance, you can include on the template a square that corresponds to the grid you have drawn on the fabric. This helps a great deal with placement of the appliqué pieces. Also, it is easier to use the negative image when drawing on freezer paper and fusible web. The positive image has its uses too, and I find it's best to have both available.

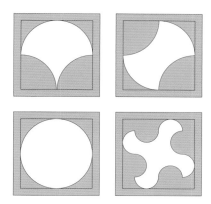

3. Referring to "Preparing the Appliqués" on page 18 and using freezer paper, prepare 21 Clamshell and 21 Counterweight patterns for invisible appliqué. Stitch in place, using the grid and negative-image template for placement. Turn over, trim the excess fabric from the background, and remove the freezer paper.

4. Referring to "Working with Fusible Web" on page 21, prepare 25 Plover and 91 Seven Treasures of Buddha pattern pieces for appliqué. Be careful with the Plover template—it has a right and wrong side. Be sure you don't turn it to the wrong side when tracing. You will be tracing it in reverse on the fusible web so that it will be correct in your quilt. I made a little multiple-copy template for the pieces needed for each Seven Treasures design. I could trace each set of four more quickly and the larger template was easier to find on my worktable. If you're wondering why there is an odd number of pieces needed for a pattern that is made up

in groups of four, look at the quilt and you'll see seven extra leaf pieces along the long edge of the triangle. You can make each one a different fabric if you want.

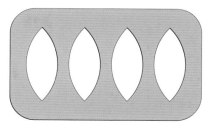

5. Using the 2½" square grid as a placement guide and your negative-image template, position the Seven Treasures of Buddha pattern pieces, with four in each square. Add the seven extra pieces along the diagonal. Fuse and stitch around the edges. I used a narrow zigzag stitch with invisible thread.

6. For the Plover design, make two extra freezer-paper templates to help you with placement. This time you will use the positive image. Trace the Plover design twice onto freezer paper, and then iron the shiny side of the paper to the shiny side of another piece of freezer paper. Cut around each template. This will give you two very sturdy templates.

7. Using the navy triangle that does not have a grid drawn on it, begin at the corner and arrange the first Plover so that it touches both drawn lines. To get the placement just right, position one freezer-paper template on each side of the Plover, like pieces of a jigsaw puzzle, making sure that they both touch a line

LAYERING AND QUILTING

1. Layer a batting square between each of the 12" appliquéd squares and a navy blue backing square, and fuse or baste.

2. Quilt as desired. I outline quilted around the appliqué pieces.

3. Trim each block to 11½" x 11½".

4. Layer a batting triangle between each of the appliquéd corner triangles and a navy blue backing triangle, and fuse or baste.

5. Quilt as desired. I outline quilted around the appliqué pieces.

6. Trim ¼" from the long edge of the triangle only. The two shorter sides will be trimmed after the quilt top is assembled and stitched.

QUILT-TOP ASSEMBLY

1. Referring to "Wide Sashing" on page 101, turn under ¼" of each blue striped sashing strip and sew the four center blocks together with sashing. Be sure to quilt the sashing strips as you go, because the narrow batting strip that is placed inside will shift very easily. Trust me, this is the voice of a sadder-but-wiser quilter speaking.

also. Leaving the freezer-paper templates in place, position the next three Plover pieces so that they fit into the templates. Then move the freezer-paper templates over so that they fit into the edges of the newly placed Plover pieces. Continue in this manner until you have all 25 Plover pieces in position.

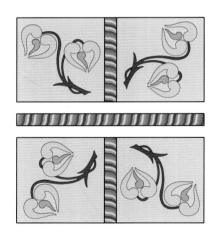

8. Fuse in place and stitch around the edges using invisible thread and a narrow zigzag stitch.

2. Find the center of the corner triangle and match it to the center of the side of the quilt. With wide sashing, sew the corner triangles to opposite corners first. Trim sashing flush with the edge of the quilt.

3. Referring to "Reversible Borders with a Contrasting Inner Border" on page 103, cut and sew a 2" x 4" piece of navy blue fabric to each end of the 2" x 27" strips of blue striped sashing. Match the two seams to the outer edge of the previously sewn sashing strips. Sew the remaining two corner triangles to the quilt. With a right-angle ruler, square up the outside edge of the quilt. Very little will be taken off—you are just "tidying up."

4. Referring to "Basic Binding" on page 107 and "Hanging Sleeves" on page 106, cut strips and bind the edges of the quilt.

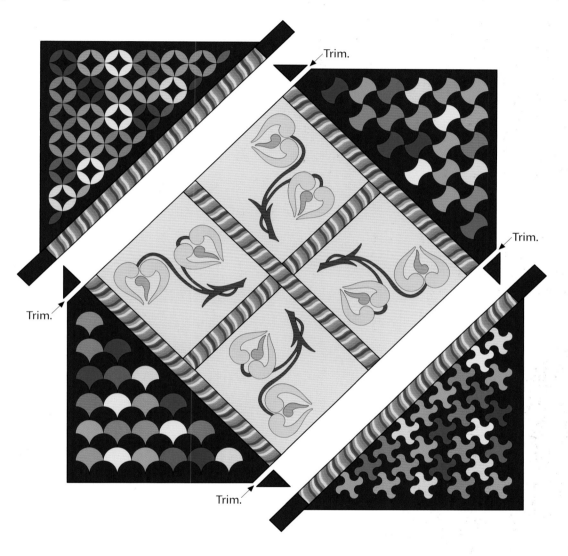

Trim.

Trim.

Trim.

Trim.

Patterns are reversed for fusible appliqué and do not include seam allowances.

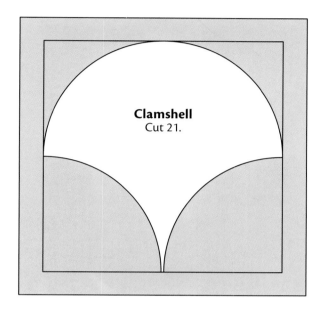

Clamshell
Cut 21.

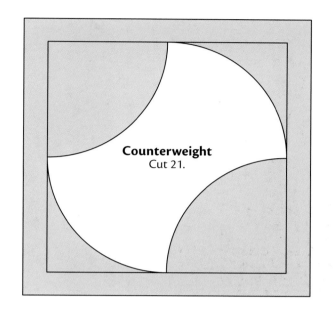

Counterweight
Cut 21.

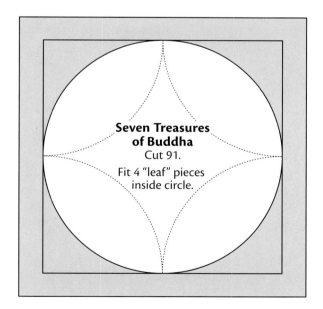

**Seven Treasures
of Buddha**
Cut 91.

Fit 4 "leaf" pieces
inside circle.

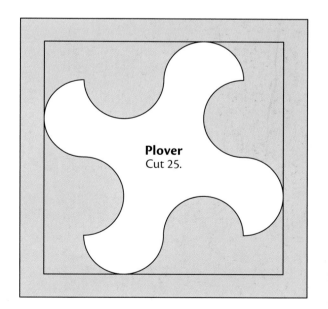

Plover
Cut 25.

Designed and made by the author

ANIMALS ON PARADE

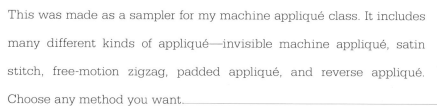

I love this cheerful quilt—bright color on black has always been a favorite combination of mine. Every season there are wonderful new animal prints to choose from, so keep your eyes open for any that would work in this setting.

This was made as a sampler for my machine appliqué class. It includes many different kinds of appliqué—invisible machine appliqué, satin stitch, free-motion zigzag, padded appliqué, and reverse appliqué. Choose any method you want.

TECHNIQUES: Multiple Techniques

Finished Quilt: 47½" x 47½"

MATERIALS

All yardages are based on 42"-wide fabric.

2⅝ yards of black fabric for background and borders

1 fat quarter (or ⅜ yard) *each* of 9 different bright prints for the frames

⅝ yard of bright multicolored print for faux piping and binding

Assorted animal prints

3 yards of fabric for backing

52" x 52" piece of batting

CUTTING

From the black fabric, cut on the lengthwise grain:

1 square, 38½" x 38½"

2 strips, 5" x 38½"

2 strips, 5" x 47½"

From *each* of the 9 bright prints, cut:

1 square, 10½" x 10½" (9 total)

From the bright multicolored print, cut:

4 strips, 1" x 38½"

5 strips, 2½" x 42"

PREPARING THE BACKGROUND

1. Make a template using the pattern on pages 88 and 89. Use it to trace and cut nine freezer-paper templates. I created mirror images of the frame for some and rotated them every which way for a varied look. To get mirror-image templates, simply layer some of your freezer paper shiny side up and some shiny side down as you are cutting.

2. Iron the freezer paper to the wrong side of the nine prints you've chosen for the frames. Referring to "Preparing the Appliqués" on page 18, prepare the frames for appliqué.

3. Using the photo on page 84 as a guide, position the nine frames on the background fabric and appliqué in place.

4. Using the appliqué method of your choice, cut out, prepare, and appliqué animal prints inside each frame. Don't forget about reverse appliqué—that's what I used for the fish. Refer to "Broderie Perse" on page 87 for additional details on using images cut from fabrics.

ADDING THE BORDERS

1. Referring to "Faux Piping" on page 104, fold the 1" x 38½" multicolored print strips in half lengthwise and press. With a ¼" seam allowance, sew them to the two sides of the background first, and then to the top and bottom.

2. Sew the 5" x 38½" border strips to the two sides of the quilt. Press toward the border. Sew the 5" x 47½" border strips to the top and bottom. Press toward the border.

FINISHING THE QUILT

1. Referring to "Layering, Basting, and Quilting" on page 105, layer the batting, backing, and quilt top together. Baste with pins, or fuse if you're using fusible batting.

2. Quilt as desired.

3. Referring to "Hanging Sleeves" on page 106, add a hanging sleeve.

4. Referring to "Basic Binding" on page 107, bind the edges of the quilt.

PADDED APPLIQUÉ

There are times when you might want to make some areas of your quilt look puffier than others. It's a simple process and can be done with the batting coming all the way out to the edge of the appliqué, as in the following heart sample, or contained inside it, as in the animal fabric in the quilt. It's best used on simpler shapes without a lot of sharp curves or points.

1. Cut a piece of polyester batting (cotton is much harder to trim later) a little larger than the area you want to pad.

2. Place the batting between the background and the appliqué piece and pin in place.

3. With thread that matches your appliqué fabric, use a walking foot to stitch as close to the edge of the appliqué piece as possible.

4. Trim the batting as close to the stitching line as you can and cover the edge with any decorative stitch you choose. Don't forget to use foundation paper.

The left side has been trimmed ready for stitching.
The right side has been satin stitched.

If the shape you are padding is contained inside a square of fabric, as in the animal prints, the only difference is that when you trim the batting from around the basting line, you will have to lift the top layer of fabric out of the way.

BRODERIE PERSE

The term *broderie perse* comes to us from France and actually means Persian embroidery, but it has also come to mean the practice of cutting printed flowers, birds, and other images from chintz or cotton and appliquéing them to a background. Originally, the reason for doing this was the extreme cost of the imported chintz fabric. It was too expensive to use, except sparingly. Even wealthy women were forced to use the fabric this way and the resulting quilts were kept for "good," so we have examples of very early quilts made using the technique.

Individual flowers or birds were cut out leaving a small seam allowance of the background fabric around the image. This was then painstakingly turned under and hand appliquéd in place. Of course now we have a faster, easier way to accomplish the same goal using fusible web.

1. Choose a fabric that has space around the image you want to appliqué. Although it is possible to use designs that overlap, it is easier when there is a bit of background fabric with no design on it.

2. Referring to "Working with Fusible Web" on page 21, remove one of the papers from a piece of Steam-A-Seam 2 and pin the sticky side to the wrong side of your fabric. Cut around the image leaving a narrow seam allowance.

3. Peel the remaining paper from the Steam-A-Seam 2 and position the appliqué piece to the background fabric. When you are pleased with the position, fuse it in place.

4. Choosing thread to match the background fabric, satin stitch around the edge of the appliqué piece. Or, if you wish, thread your machine with invisible thread and zigzag stitch around the edge.

The monkey from "Animals on Parade" was done using the *broderie perse* technique. It was printed on a black background, so I chose black thread to zigzag stitch around it

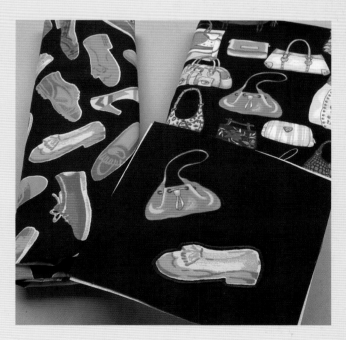

Another advantage to *broderie perse* is the ability to combine images from different fabrics to create the look you want. Here I combined a purse from one fabric with a shoe from another. You can have fun combining animals and other images for "Animals on Parade."

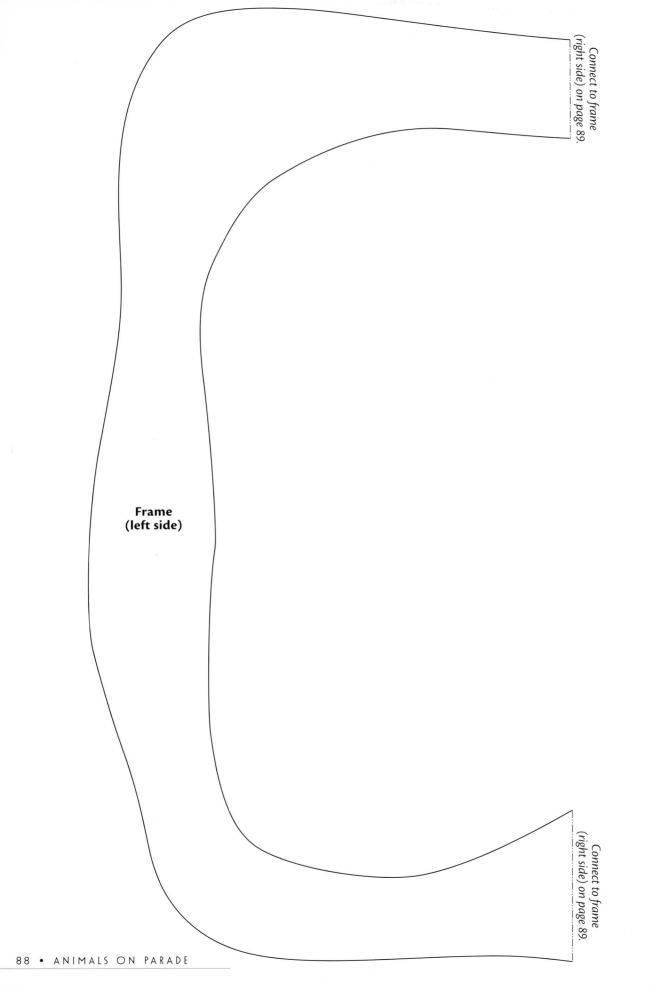

**Frame
(left side)**

Connect to frame
(right side) on page 89.

Connect to frame
(right side) on page 89.

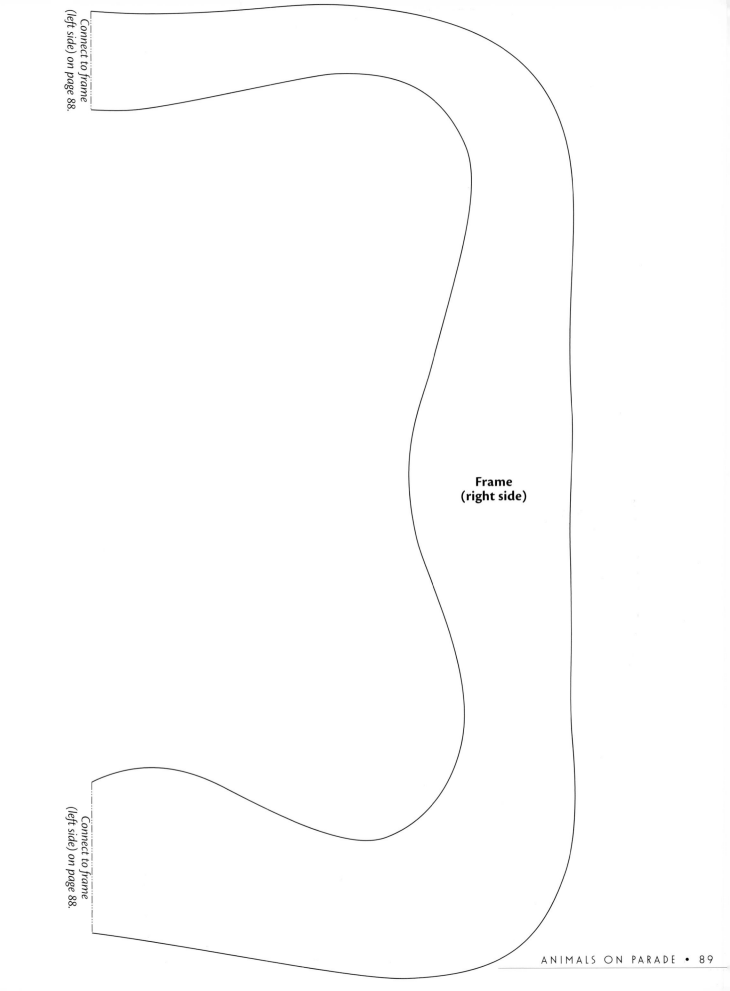

Connect to frame (left side) on page 88.

Connect to frame (left side) on page 88.

Frame (right side)

Designed and made by Carol Seeley

CHRISTMAS IS

The area where I live has a wealth of talented quilters and quilt teachers, including my friend Carol Seeley, the 2007 Canadian Teacher of the Year award winner. Carol had designed and made this terrific Christmas quilt a few years ago, and when I asked her if I could use it in my book, she said yes.

Carol combined a lovely pieced block and an original appliqué design for this quilt, and then added an innovative border. All in all, it is a great example of the kind of teaching samples she provides for her students.

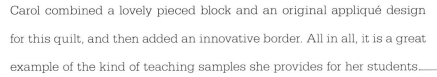

TECHNIQUES: Invisible Machine Appliqué, Fusible Appliqué

Finished Quilt: 40" x 40"

MATERIALS

All yardages are based on 42"-wide fabric.

1⅓ yards of white tone-on-tone fabric for background

1⅓ yards of green Christmas print for border

1 yard of green print for leaves, vines, pieced block, and binding

½ yard *total* of assorted red prints for pieced block, appliquéd flowers, and berries

1⅜ yards of fabric for backing

42" x 42" piece of batting

4½ yards of purchased gold lamé piping

CUTTING

From the assorted red prints, cut:
2 strips, 1½" x 42"; cut 28 diamonds*
1 square, 1¾" x 1¾"

From the green print, cut:
2 squares, 2⅞" x 2⅞"; cut each square once diagonally to yield 4 half-square triangles
5 strips, 2½" x 42"

From the white tone-on-tone fabric, cut:
4 squares, 18½" x 18½"
4 rectangles, 1¾" x 4"
4 squares, 2" x 2"
2 squares, 3¼" x 3¼"; cut each square twice diagonally to yield 8 quarter-square triangles

From the green Christmas print, cut:
1 square, 40" x 40"

See "Cutting Diamonds" on page 92.

CUTTING DIAMONDS

Cut the diamonds using either a template or a rotary-cutting ruler with a 45° line.

Using a template. Make a template using the diamond pattern on page 98, including the seam allowance. Cut 28 diamonds from the 1½" red strips.

Using a ruler. Align the 45° line of the ruler with the top edge of a 1½" red strip as shown. Cut along the edge of the ruler to establish your diagonal line. Rotate the strip 180°. Position the ruler so that the 45° line of the ruler is again along the top edge of the strip; align the angled edge of the strip with the 1½" line of the ruler. Cut. Repeat to cut 28 diamonds.

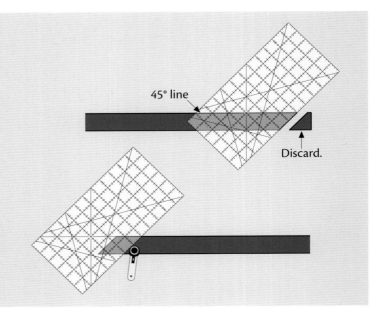

MAKING THE PIECED BLOCKS

1. On the wrong side of one red diamond, mark the intersection of the ¼" seams at the wide (135°) angle on each diamond. With right sides together, and starting from the sharply pointed end (45° angle), sew to the intersection of the drawn lines and back-stitch. Press seams open. Repeat with another pair of diamonds.

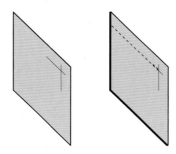

2. In the same manner, sew the two pairs of diamonds together. Press seams open. Make four of these units.

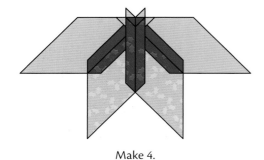

Make 4.

3. Find the center of the long side of one green triangle by gently folding and finger-pressing to mark it. Pin to the center of the red diamond unit. Sew from raw edge to raw edge. Press the seam toward the green triangle.

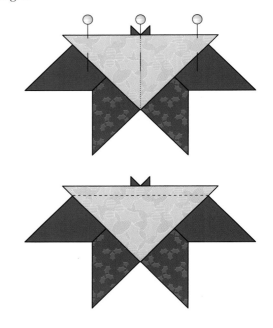

4. Mark a spot ¼" in from both sides of one corner on the 2" white squares. Mark the right-angle corner of the white triangles in the same way.

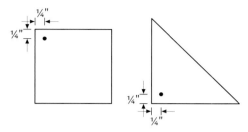

5. Place a white triangle on a red diamond, right sides together. Stitch from the pointed end up to the marked point and backstitch.

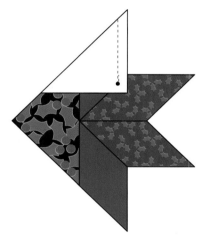

6. Remove from the machine and pivot the triangle so that it is aligned with the edge of the next diamond. Pin and insert the needle right next to the last stitch. You will begin sewing from the right-angle corner. Reduce your stitch length to almost zero and anchor your stitches. Increase the stitch length to normal and stitch to the outer edge.

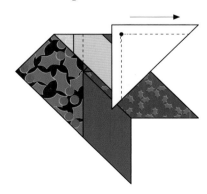

7. Repeat steps 5 and 6 to sew a triangle to the opposite side of the diamond unit.

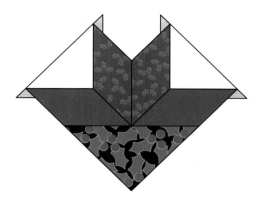

8. Use the same stitch-and-pivot technique to stitch a white square in place between the center diamonds. Make four of these units.

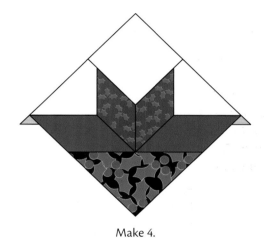

Make 4.

9. Sew a 1¾" x 4" white rectangle between each pair of diamond units as shown. Press seams toward the diamond units. Sew the red 1¾" square between two remaining white rectangles and press seams toward the red square. Sew the units together. Trim points. Your block should measure 8½" x 8½". Trim, if necessary, to square up your block, leaving ¼" beyond the points.

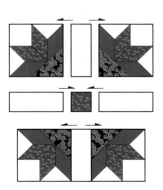

MAKING THE APPLIQUÉ BLOCKS

Two kinds of appliqué are used in this quilt—both done by machine, of course. The red berries will be fused and stitched with a narrow zigzag stitch around the outside edge, and everything else will be done with edges turned under. You may want to review "Invisible Machine Appliqué" on page 16 and "Working with Fusible Web" on page 21 before you start.

I always like to work on small pieces whenever I can, so for this piece I recommend doing as much of the appliqué as possible on the 18½" background squares before sewing them together with the pieced block. You'll be able to appliqué everything except the small section of vine and the four berries that overlap the seam lines.

1. Referring to "Making Stems" on page 42, prepare eight bias stems that are 16" long and four that are 2½" long. On each background square, mark the point 8¼" in from the right side and 8" up from the bottom as shown in the placement guide below. This marks the center of the flower. Tape the long stems in place. The short stems will be sewn on after the corner squares are sewn to the center block.

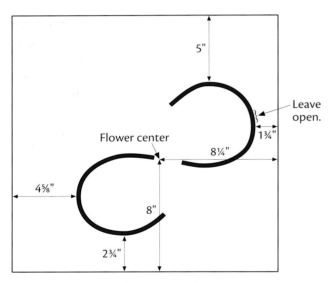

Stem placement guide

2. Referring to "Stitching the Appliqué" on page 19, stitch the inner curves of the stems first, then the outer ones. Leave an area open where indicated so that you can tuck in the short stem sections after the background squares have been sewn together.

3. Refer to "Preparing the Appliqués" on page 18 to make freezer-paper templates for the flowers, leaves, and flower centers using the patterns on page 98. Prepare a total of 20 leaves (8 of which are reversed), four large flowers, four medium flowers, and four flower centers.

4. Center the flower over the marked point. Stitch the large flowers first, followed by the medium flowers, and then the flower centers, removing freezer paper as you go. Stitch the leaves.

5. Referring to "Working with Fusible Web" on page 21, prepare 80 berries using the pattern on page 98. Referring to the placement diagram below, position the large clusters of berries, making sure you cover the raw edge of each stem. When you have them where you want them, fuse them in place. With invisible thread in your needle, stitch in place using a very narrow zigzag stitch. The small clusters will be added after the blocks are sewn together.

Appliqué placement

SEWING THE BLOCKS TOGETHER

1. Cut one corner off each 18½" square by measuring 5¾" along the two adjacent, marked edges of the square. Use a ruler and rotary cutter to make the cut.

Note: It's important that your pieced block measures exactly 8½" square. If it doesn't, you will need to use different measurements for cutting off the corner. For an 8¼" block, measure 5½" along your 18½" square; for an 8¾" block, measure 5⅞".

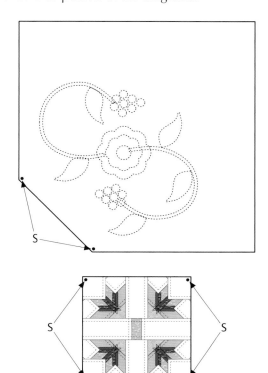

2. On each 18½" background piece and on the pieced center block, mark the points where the ¼" seam lines will intersect on the wrong sides of the fabric. These are shown as point S in the diagrams.

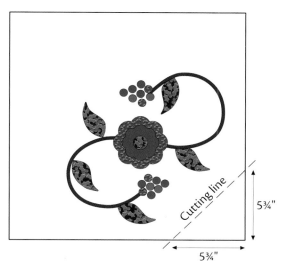

3. Sew an appliquéd background piece to each side of the pieced center block, right sides together, lining up the S points on the square to the center block. Pin through the S points. Begin and end the stitching at an S point, anchoring your stitches at both ends. Do not stitch to the edge of the fabric. Repeat for all four sides of the center block.

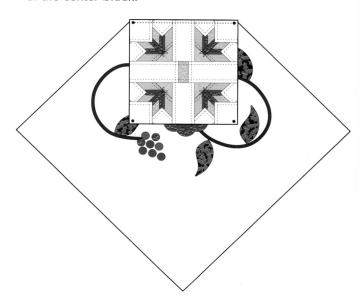

4. To stitch the sides of the background squares to each other, begin at the S point, anchor your stitches, and stitch to the outer edge of the square. Be careful not to catch the center block in the seam. Repeat for all four sides. Your quilt top should now measure 36½" x 36½".

FINISHING THE APPLIQUÉ

1. Cut 12 freezer-paper templates using the inner line on the diamond pattern on page 98. Prepare the appliqués using red fabric.

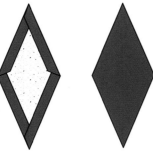

Make 12.

2. Referring to the photo on page 90 for placement, center the 12 red diamonds between the pieced diamonds, with the points just touching the inner corners of the pieced diamonds. Stitch in place and remove the freezer paper.

3. Referring to the placement guide on page 94 and the photograph on page 90, position the four small stem pieces, tucking them into the openings left for them. Stitch in place, including the opening left in the longer stem piece.

4. Position four berries at the end of each short stem and fuse in place. Stitch them as you did the larger clusters.

ADDING THE BORDER

1. Fold the 40" x 40" square of border fabric in half lengthwise and press. Without unfolding, fold it again in the other direction and press.

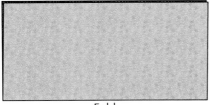

Fold

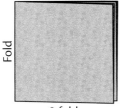

2 folds

2. Fold once more in half diagonally. This last fold must be from the center of the border fabric out to the corners. If you have folded it correctly, you will have one side—and one side only—that does not have folds.

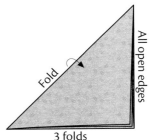

3. Make a paper pattern of the curved border pattern on page 99 and lay it along the open side. Trace the pattern onto the fabric. Cut along the curved line.

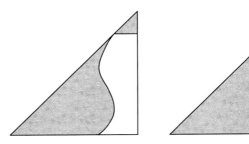

4. Unfold, and save the center piece for another project. Pick a spot on the curved edge of the border that is fairly straight and align the raw edge of the purchased gold lamé piping even with the raw edge of the border. Leave a 3" tail, and with the zipper foot on your machine, stitch the piping to the border. Clip the seam allowance of the piping when necessary. Clip all the way to the stitching line when sewing the inner points at the four corners.

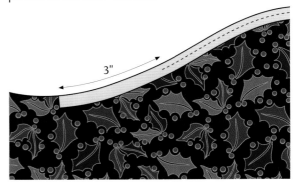

5. Once you are almost back to the starting point, you will need to join the ends of the piping. Open up the piping, cut the cording so that the ends butt together, and overlap the lamé fabric. Fold under the end of the lamé so you will not have a raw edge. Continue stitching the piping until you overlap the first stitches.

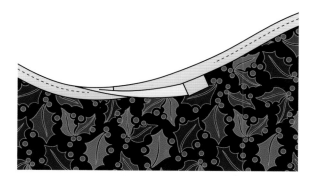

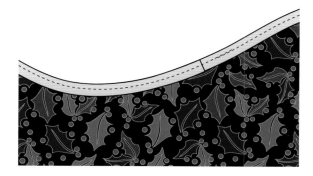

6. Fold the raw edge of the piping toward the wrong side of the border; press lightly to keep it in place, being careful not to melt the lamé.

7. Center the border over the quilt top, matching the centers of the border to the seam lines of the appliquéd quilt center. Pin well and stitch in place using the zipper foot on your machine. Use either a matching thread color or invisible thread.

8. Trim excess fabric behind the border if desired, and square up the quilt top if necessary.

FINISHING THE QUILT

1. Referring to "Layering, Basting, and Quilting" on page 105, layer the batting, backing, and quilt top together. Baste with pins, or fuse if you're using fusible batting.

2. Quilt as desired.

3. Referring to "Hanging Sleeves" on page 106, add a hanging sleeve.

4. Referring to "Basic Binding" on page 107, bind your quilt with the green strips.

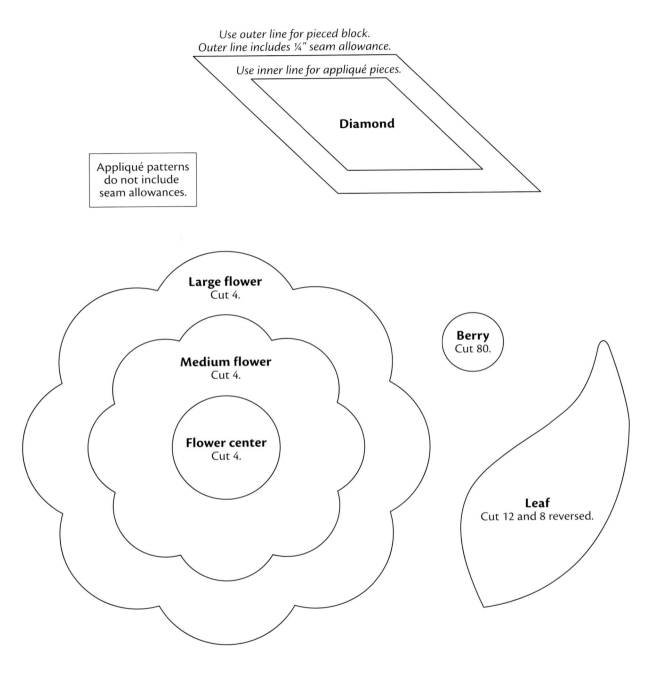

Use outer line for pieced block.
Outer line includes ¼" seam allowance.

Use inner line for appliqué pieces.

Diamond

Appliqué patterns
do not include
seam allowances.

Large flower
Cut 4.

Medium flower
Cut 4.

Flower center
Cut 4.

Berry
Cut 80.

Leaf
Cut 12 and 8 reversed.

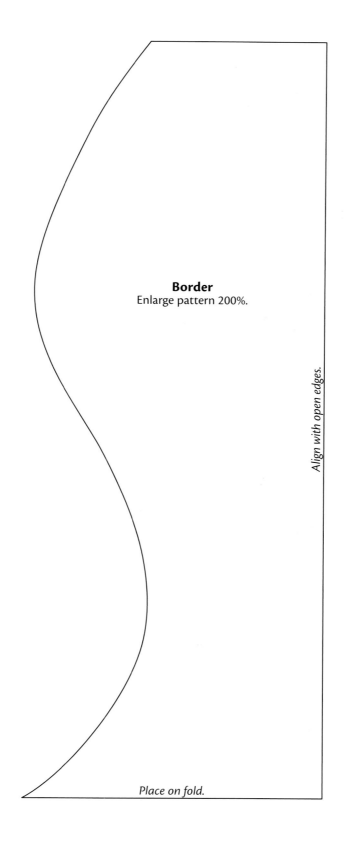

Border
Enlarge pattern 200%.

Align with open edges.

Place on fold.

When your blocks are appliquéd, you're ready to stitch them together, add borders, and finish your quilt. In this section I've included basic instructions for the quilts in this book, whether you make your quilt in the traditional manner or use the reversible technique.

ABOUT REVERSIBLE BLOCKS AND SASHING

As I have mentioned, I like to work with small units or blocks so that I can pivot them easily while quilting and avoid having to struggle with the whole quilt passing through the machine. To make a quilt this way, you create and quilt the blocks, trim them to the size indicated in each project, and then join them with sashing strips. It is possible to create two completely different sides, as I did in "Crazy Hearts" on page 33, or if you'd rather not bother with anything fancy on the back you can use any backing fabric you want.

BASIC SASHING

Basic sashing is used to join blocks that have already been quilted. The components are first joined into rows, and then the rows are sewn together. Basic sashing is also used to join a quilted border to a quilt. You can use a narrow sashing that finishes to ⅝" wide, or you can go wider if that is more in proportion with your quilt blocks. You will need sashing fabric for both the front and the back of your quilt.

1. Cut 1⅛"-wide strips from the sashing fabric for the back, and cut 1¾"-wide strips from the sashing fabric for the front. Cut across the full width of your fabric.

2. Fold the 1¾" strips in half lengthwise, wrong sides together, and press.

3. Using the full length of the strips, on side A (the front of the quilt), align the raw edges of the folded strip with the raw edge of the first block to be joined. On side B (the back side of the quilt), align the raw edge of the 1⅛"-wide strip with the raw edge of the same block,

right sides together. Sew both sashing strips to the first block with a ¼" seam. You will sew both sashing strips to the same block at the same time.

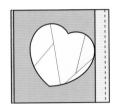

4. Trim the ends of the strips even with the top and bottom of the block.

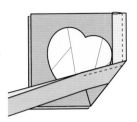

5. Sew the second block to the raw edge of the 1⅛"-wide strip, right sides together. The edges of the two seam allowances should meet in the middle of the sashing strip and fill the space between the two blocks. If there is a gap between the two edges, increase your seam allowance; if the two edges overlap, decrease your seam allowance.

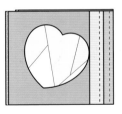

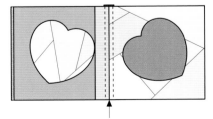

Raw edges should meet.

6. Continue sewing sashing strips between the blocks until you finish the row. You now have three of the four edges of the sashing strips sewn by machine. Pin the last remaining part of the sashing (the folded strip) in place, covering the machine stitching. Sew the remaining edge using the invisible zigzag stitch described on page 16, or sew it by hand if you prefer.

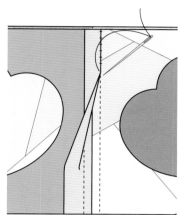

7. To join the rows or to add a border, follow the same directions as for joining block to block but use longer sashing strips. If you need to piece sashing strips, sew the ends together with a diagonal seam. Trim the excess fabric and press the seam open.

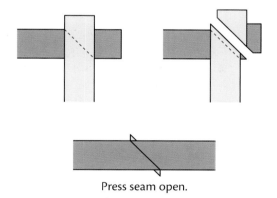

Press seam open.

8. When joining horizontal rows of blocks, be sure to line up the vertical strips between the blocks from one row to the next.

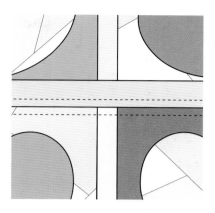

9. To add borders to a reversible quilt, refer to "Reversible Borders" on page 103.

WIDE SASHING

Two quilts in this book feature wider sashing: "Xs and Os" on page 39, and "Sashiko Revisited" on page 77. I think you'll agree that neither of them would have looked right with narrow sashing. (By the way, it is perfectly acceptable to use wide sashing in one part of the quilt and narrow sashing in another.)

1. To make wider sashing, first decide how wide you want it to be and cut strips that size plus ½". On the sashing fabric you have chosen for the front of your quilt, turn under ¼" toward the wrong side of one long side and press.

2. With right sides together, align the raw edge (the edge that does not have ¼" turned under) of the sashing with the raw edge of the front side of the block. Underneath, align the raw edge of the other sashing fabric with the raw edge of the block, right sides together.

3. Sew both pieces of sashing to the same block at the same time with ¼" seam allowance.

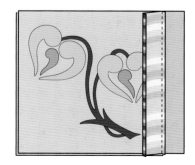

4. Sew the next block to the sashing strip that doesn't have the edge turned under. Measure the distance between the resulting seam allowances and cut a strip of batting that wide. Lay the batting in the space and cover with the sashing fabric with the folded edge. Hand or machine stitch the folded edge down.

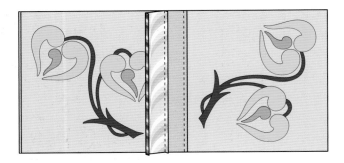

5. To hold the batting in place you must quilt the sashing strip, and I strongly recommend doing it as you go.

ABOUT BORDERS

Entire books have been written about quilt borders, so I hope you realize that the options discussed here are just a few of the many possibilities out there. The quilts in this book illustrate five different ways of putting on borders.

BASIC BORDERS

1. Measure the length of your quilt through the center and mark the centers. Cut two strips to that measurement, piecing if necessary.

2. Center the border strip with the center of the quilt and sew with a ¼" seam. Press the seams toward the borders.

Measure center of quilt,
top to bottom. Mark centers.

3. Measure the width of your quilt through the center and mark the centers. Cut two strips to that measurement, piecing if necessary.

4. Center the border strip with the center of the quilt and sew with a ¼" seam. Press the seams toward the borders.

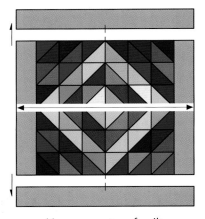

Measure center of quilt,
side to side, including border
strips. Mark centers.

REVERSIBLE BORDERS

1. Measure the length of your quilt through the center. Add an extra 1" in both directions to allow for slippage when quilting.

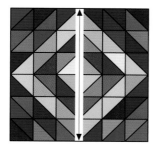

For borders, measure
through center of quilt.

2. Cut border strips for the right and left sides of the quilt for both the front and back, according to your measurements. Cut strips of batting the same size.

3. Pin or fuse the three layers together: front border strip, batting, and backing border strip.

4. Quilt as desired.

5. Trim to the desired length and width, leaving ½" for seam allowances.

6. Join border strips to the sides of the quilt with sashing strips as for sewing blocks and rows together (see "Basic Sashing" on page 100).

7. Measure the width through the center, add an extra 1" in both directions, and repeat steps 2–6 to add the top and bottom borders.

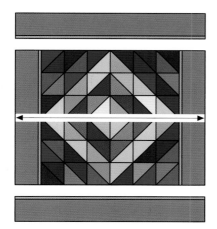

REVERSIBLE BORDERS WITH A CONTRASTING INNER BORDER

In "Crazy Hearts" on page 33, you can see an example of a reversible border with what looks like a contrasting inner border. That inner border is really the sashing that was used to join the already-quilted border to the quilt.

To create this effect, join the top and bottom border strips to the quilt using contrasting fabric for the sashing. Before joining the side borders to the quilt, sew a rectangle of border fabric to each end of the sashing strips for the sides (see "Basic Sashing" on page 100). Sew the side border pieces to the quilt with the pieced sashing strips.

TERRE'S BORDERS (BORDERS WITHOUT SASHING)

If you'd like to have the ease of adding a border to your already-quilted top without the intrusion of a sashing strip, here's the perfect method. I learned this wonderful technique from a student in New Braunfels, Texas. Terre shared it with us in class, and with her permission, I am sharing it with you. Anything that adds to my repertoire of borders is a welcome option. I used her method in "Xs and Os" on page 39.

1. Measure the length of the quilt through the center from top to bottom. Cut two side borders to that length from the border fabric for the front and the fabric for the back. Piece strips together if necessary. Mark the center of the borders and the quilt.

2. With right sides together, place the front border strip on the top of the quilt, matching the centers and aligning raw edges. Pin in place. Place the back border strip, right sides together, on the back of the quilt, matching the center and aligning raw edges. Reposition the pins. Stitch in place with a ¼" seam allowance. Remove the pins, but do not press or open the borders outward.

3. Cut two strips of batting the same length as the borders, but ¼" narrower in width. Position a strip of batting right up against the raw edge of the seam allowance you just sewed, butting the edges together. Sew the batting strip to the seam allowance of the quilt using a "Lycra" or "serpentine" stitch on your machine and a neutral thread color.

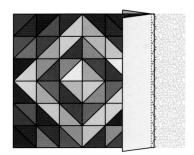

4. Fold both border pieces over the batting. Fuse the three layers together if using fusible batting, or pin the layers of traditional batting. I usually sew all four borders on before doing the quilting, so I baste the raw edges together to keep them from coming "unfused" while the other borders are being sewn on. Repeat the procedure for the opposite border.

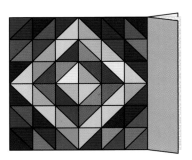

5. Measure the width of your quilt through the center to cut the border strips for the top and bottom of your quilt. Repeat steps 2–4.

FAUX PIPING

I love the look of a very narrow inner border and often include this little ¼" folded accent piece to set off a wider border. I once tried to create a ¼" border on a quilt by sewing a ¾" strip of fabric to it and discovered that it's almost impossible to sew something that narrow without getting all sorts of wobbly bits. So, when I discovered that you can get it straight by sewing a folded strip to the quilt top as faux piping, instead of sewing a very narrow border on, I was off and running.

1. Cut strips of fabric 1" by whatever length you need to cover the sides of your quilt. Fold in half lengthwise and press.

2. Aligning the raw edges of the folded strip with the raw edge of the quilt, sew with a scant ¼" seam. Repeat on the opposite side of your quilt. Trim ends flush with the edge of the quilt. Do not press.

Folded edge of faux piping   Folded edge of faux piping

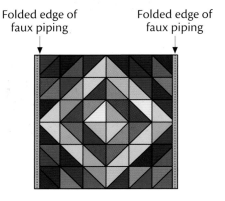

3. Repeat on the remaining two sides of your quilt.

4. Sew the borders on in the same order. Place the first border strip on top of the piping right sides together and pin in place. Turn the quilt over so you can see the stitching line for the faux piping, and stitch just inside it. This ensures that the stitching line for the faux piping will not show on the top of the quilt. Press the seam toward the border.

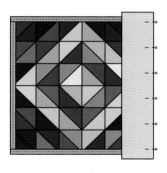

Back of quilt

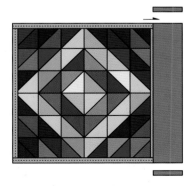

5. Continue adding the borders in the same order as the faux piping.

LAYERING, BASTING, AND QUILTING

How you baste your quilt together is very much a matter of personal preference. I'm in love with fusible batting, but I know some quilters would rather not use it. You can baste with safety pins or use a spray adhesive for machine quilting.

When the quilt top is complete and any quilting designs you are planning have been marked, assemble the quilt sandwich: the backing, batting, and quilt top. The backing and batting should be at least 4" larger than the quilt top. If your quilt is larger than the fabric width, you will have to piece the backing either horizontally or vertically, whichever makes the most efficient use of your fabric.

1. Spread the backing, wrong side up, on a flat, clean surface. (If you are using fusible batting, protect the tabletop with an old blanket.) Anchor the backing fabric with masking tape or binder clips. Be careful not to pull it too tight or stretch it out of shape.

2. Spread the batting over the backing, smoothing out any wrinkles. It helps if you take the batting out of the package and unroll it the day before you need it.

3. Center the pressed quilt top, right side up, on top of the batting. Smooth out any wrinkles and make sure the edges of the quilt top are parallel to the edges of the backing.

4. To baste the layers together, use No. 2 rustproof safety pins for machine quilting. Begin in the center and place pins in a grid about 6" to 8" apart. If you are using a fusible batting, fuse the layers together following the manufacturer's directions.

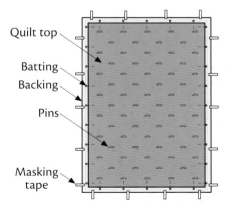

Quilt top

Batting

Backing

Pins

Masking tape

5. For machine-guided quilting, use your walking foot. For free-motion quilting, drop the feed dogs and attach a darning foot to stitch the designs. Maurine Noble's *Machine Quilting Made Easy* (Martingale & Company, 1994) is a great resource if you'd like more information about machine quilting.

HANGING SLEEVES

For quilts that you expect to display on a wall or in a show, prepare a hanging sleeve to attach as you sew the binding on. Most shows require a 4" sleeve, so if you are planning to enter your quilt in a show it's best to make one that size even if it seems too big for the quilt.

1. Measure the width of your quilt and subtract 1". From the backing fabric, or something similar to it, cut a piece 9" wide by that measurement and fold the ends under to make a hem. Stitch the hems.

2. Before pinning the sleeve to the quilt top, press it lengthwise, wrong sides together, with one side extending ½" above the other. This will put a crease in the bottom of the sleeve that will be hand stitched to the back of the quilt. You want the sleeve to have enough ease to hold a hanging rod without making a bulge in the front of the quilt.

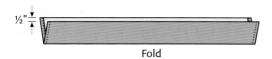

Fold

3. Line up the raw edges of the sleeve with the top of the quilt, making sure the shorter portion is toward the back, and machine baste in place.

Baste sleeve to top edge of quilt.

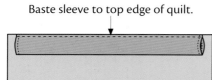

4. The top of the sleeve will be machine sewn in with the binding, but the bottom must be hand stitched to the back of the quilt. When you do the hand stitching push the top layer of the hanging sleeve up so that the crease you put in is visible along the bottom. Pin and blindstitch the sleeve to the back of your quilt along the crease. There will be plenty of room for the rod.

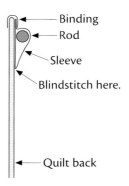

Binding — Rod — Sleeve — Blindstitch here. — Quilt back

BINDING

I've heard quilters say they hate putting binding on a quilt, and I remember a time when I felt that way myself. But now I love that part, for two reasons: first, the quilt is finished—always a good feeling!—and second, I know how to do it so that I'm pleased with the results. Way back when I dreaded that part of quilting it was because I didn't know how to do it "right." For many of us, that's a word that conjures up images of a person with a scorecard handing out test results, and I don't think we should feel that way about any aspect of quilting. You decide which way is the right way and don't let anybody tell you you're doing it wrong. Here are two ways that I do it, but take what you like from the instructions and leave the rest.

BASIC BINDING

This is how I do it when a single binding fabric will look good on both sides of the quilt.

1. From the width of the fabric, cut enough 2½"-wide strips to go around the quilt plus about 4" extra for joining strips and turning corners. Join the strips end to end using a diagonal seam to make a continuous strip.

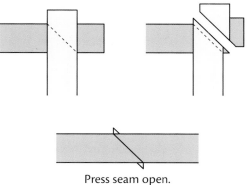

Press seam open.

2. Fold the strip in half lengthwise, wrong sides together, and press.

3. Put the walking foot on your machine.

4. Starting at a corner and leaving a 2" tail, match the raw edges of the binding with the raw edges of the quilt. Beginning ¼" from the corner, anchor your stitches and sew the binding to the first side of the quilt with a ¼"-wide seam allowance. Stop ¼" from the corner and again anchor your stitches.

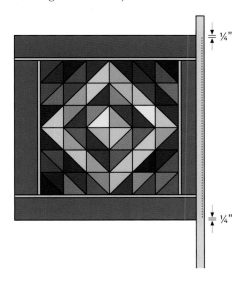

5. Remove the quilt from the machine. Draw a perpendicular line from the stitching line (A) to the fold (C). I call this the baseline.

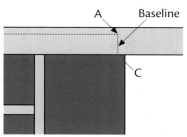

6. Measure the distance from the stitching line to the folded edge of your binding strip. It should be 1". Find the center of the baseline (it should be ½" from the folded edge and ½" from the stitching line) and make a mark. From that mark, measure ½" to the right of the baseline, and make another mark (B). Draw a line from points A and C to point B to form a triangle.

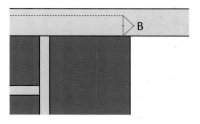

7. Fold the binding under at point B as shown. Pin in place. If you can't see the triangle you've just drawn and the folded edges are not aligned, it's folded the wrong way. Fold the quilt back out of the way and starting with the needle at point A, anchor your stitches. Then sew to point B, pivot, and sew to point C; anchor your stitches. Do not sew across the baseline.

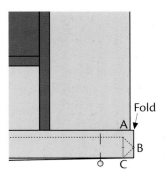

8. Remove the quilt from the machine and align the binding with the edge of the next side of the quilt. Mark the point at which you start stitching point D; this is under point A (and ¼" from the edge). With the needle at point D, anchor your stitches and then sew to ¼" from the next corner; anchor your stitches.

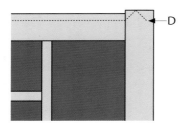

9. Repeat steps 5–8 for the second and third corners. On the fourth side, sew to where you started (¼" from the end of side 4); anchor your stitches. Draw the ABC triangle as you did for the previous three corners, but instead of folding the binding under, pin it to the tail you left at the beginning, aligning the folded edges.

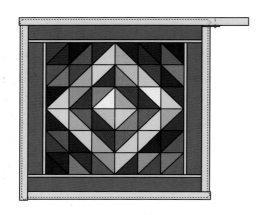

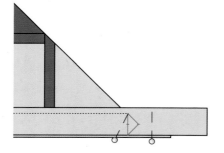

10. Sew the triangle through both pieces of binding, thereby enclosing the ends in the corner seam.

11. Trim the corners from each triangle and turn right side out. This will give you a sewn-down mitered corner on both sides of your quilt.

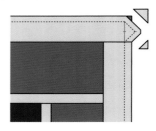

12. Turn the binding to the reverse side and hand or machine sew the folded edge to the quilt.

Back side

REVERSIBLE BINDING

Use this method if you have made a reversible quilt and you want the binding to be different on the front and back. The binding will be sewn to the sides first, and then to the top and bottom.

There's another scenario in which this technique is helpful: when you want a particular fabric for the binding but you don't have quite enough to cut 2½"-wide strips. Since you can use 1⅛"-wide strips on one side of the reversible binding, you might have enough of that special fabric if you follow these steps.

1. From the width of the fabric, cut enough 1⅛"-wide strips to go around the quilt plus a few inches for the corners. Cut strips for the other side 1¾" wide. If the sides are longer than 40", join strips end to end as instructed in step 1 of "Basic Binding" on page 107.

2. Fold the 1¾"-wide strip in half lengthwise, wrong sides together, and press.

3. With right sides together and matching raw edges, sew the single layer of binding and the folded layer of binding together with a ¼" seam allowance. You will be sewing through three layers.

4. Press the seam open. This helps the binding fold at the midpoint when you attach the binding to the quilt.

5. Sew the binding to opposite sides of the quilt first. With right sides together and raw edges matching, sew the single layer of binding to one side of the quilt (the front if you are working with 1⅛" strips of a special, limited fabric). Trim the ends even with the quilt. Fold the binding at the seam line and hand or machine sew the folded edge to the other side of the quilt. I sew by machine using the same stitch I use for invisible machine appliqué (see page 16).

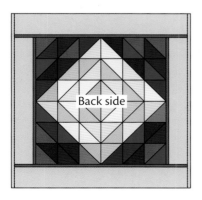

6. Leaving a ½" tail at the beginning and end, sew the single layer of binding to the top and bottom of the quilt.

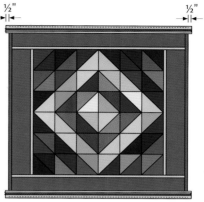

7. With right sides together, sew the ends of the binding flush with the ends of the quilt. Make sure you keep the folded edge lined up with the folded edge of the seam allowance you have just sewn. Trim the seam allowance and turn right sides out.

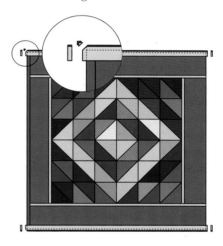

8. Hand or machine sew the folded edge to the reverse side of the quilt as you did with the first two sides.

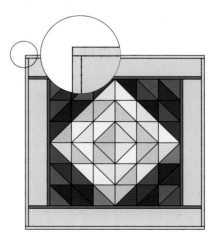

RESOURCES

BERNINA
www.bernina.com
Sewing machines and specialty feet

COME QUILT WITH ME INC.
www.comequiltwithme.com
Brooklyn Revolver

DOVER PUBLICATIONS
store.doverpublications.com
Japanese Design Motifs: 4,260 Illustrations of Japanese Crests compiled by the Matsuya Piece-Goods Store, translated by Fumie Adachi

THE ELECTRIC QUILT COMPANY
www.electricquilt.com
Quilting software

HOBBS BONDED FIBERS
www.hobbsbondedfibers.com
Hobbs Heirloom Cotton Batting, Hobbs Fusible Batting, and Hobbs Organic Cotton (with Scrim) Batting

HTCW INC.
www.htcwproducts.net
Fun-dation foundation paper

MARTINGALE & COMPANY
www.martingale-pub.com
Machine Quilting Made Easy (1994) by Maurine Noble; *Reversible Quilts* (2002), *More Reversible Quilts* (2004), and *Sensational Sashiko: Japanese Appliqué and Quilting by Machine* (2005), all by Sharon Pederson; and *Color for the Terrified Quilter* (2007) by Sharon Pederson and Ionne McCauley.

SHARON PEDERSON
www.sharonquilts.com
Acrylic templates for "Double Wedding Ring"

THE WARM COMPANY
www.warmcompany.com
Steam-A-Seam 2

YLI CORPORATION
www.ylicorp.com
Thread and the brochure "A Thread of Truth"

ABOUT THE AUTHOR

Photo by Sandra Chow

In high school, Sharon's aptitude tests pegged her as "mechanical." Images of sliding under a car with a wrench in her hand and grease in her hair flashed through her mind; she quickly enrolled in all the nonmechanical courses she could find. Little did she know that she just had to meet the right kind of machine to realize her mechanical potential.

Her motto is that if you can sew it by hand, you can sew it by machine, and you should have fun doing it. This love affair with sewing machines is an ongoing one, and she is never happier than when sitting at one of her two wonderful Berninas.

Teaching others to love using their machines is another thing Sharon enjoys, and a large part of her life is now spent on the road traveling from one quilting event to another. The publication of her four previous books, *Reversible Quilts, More Reversible Quilts, Sensational Sashiko: Japanese Appliqué and Quilting by Machine,* and *Color for the Terrified Quilter* with Ionne McCauley (all published by Martingale & Company), has made sure she is on the road a lot.

When not sewing or traveling to teach, Sharon enjoys cooking, reading, long walks on the beach, and movies.

She and her husband are still living happily ever after in a little house in the woods on Vancouver Island, British Columbia.

Sharon invites you to visit her Web site at www.sharonquilts.com.

NEW AND BESTSELLING TITLES FROM

America's Best-Loved Craft & Hobby Books®
America's Best-Loved Knitting Books®

America's Best-Loved Quilt Books®

APPLIQUÉ
Adoration Quilts

Beautiful Blooms—*New!*
Cutting-Garden Quilts
Favorite Quilts from Anka's Treasures
Mimi Dietrich's Favorite Applique Quilts
Sunbonnet Sue and Scottie Too

FOCUS ON WOOL
The Americana Collection
Needle-Felting Magic
Needle Felting with Cotton and Wool—*New!*
Simply Primitive

GENERAL QUILTMAKING
Bits and Pieces
Bound for Glory
Calendar Kids
Charmed
Christmas with Artful Offerings
Colorful Quilts
Comfort and Joy
Cool Girls Quilt
Creating Your Perfect Quilting Space
A Dozen Roses
Fig Tree Quilts: Houses
**Follow-the-Line Quilting Designs
    Volume Three—*New!***
The Little Box of Quilter's Chocolate Desserts
More Reversible Quilts
Points of View
Positively Postcards
Prairie Children and Their Quilts
Quilt Revival
Quilter's Block-a-Day Calendar
Quilter's Happy Hour—New!
Quilting in the Country
Reversible Quilts
Sensational Sashiko
Simple Seasons
Simple Seasons Recipe Cards
Simple Traditions
Skinny Quilts and Table Runners—*New!*
Twice Quilted
Young at Heart Quilts

LEARNING TO QUILT
Color for the Terrified Quilter
Happy Endings, Revised Edition
Let's Quilt!
Your First Quilt Book (or it should be!)
Machine Quilting Made Easy

PAPER PIECING
300 Paper-Pieced Quilt Blocks
Easy Machine Paper Piecing
Paper-Pieced Mini Quilts
Show Me How to Paper Piece
Showstopping Quilts to Foundation Piece
Spellbinding Quilts

PIECING
40 Fabulous Quick-Cut Quilts
Better by the Dozen
Big 'n Easy
Clever Quarters, Too
Copy Cat Quilts—*New!*
Maple Leaf Quilts—*New!*
Mosaic Picture Quilts
New Cuts for New Quilts
Nine by Nine
Quilts on the Double—*New!*
Ribbon Star Quilts—*New!*
Sew Fun, Sew Colorful Quilts
Sew One and You're Done
Snowball Quilts
Square Deal
Sudoku Quilts
Wheel of Mystery Quilts

QUILTS FOR BABIES & CHILDREN
Baby Wraps—*New!*
Even More Quilts for Baby
Lickety-Split Quilts for Little Ones
The Little Box of Baby Quilts
Quilts from the Heart
Quilts for Baby
Sweet and Simple Baby Quilts

SCRAP QUILTS
Nickel Quilts
Save the Scraps
Simple Strategies for Scrap Quilt

CRAFTS
101 Sparkling Necklaces
Art from the Heart
The Beader's Handbook
Card Design
Creative Embellishments
Crochet for Beaders
It's a Wrap
It's in the Details
The Little Box of Beaded Bracelets
    and Earrings
The Little Box of Beaded Necklaces
    and Earrings
Miniature Punchneedle Embroidery
A Passion for Punchneedle
Punchneedle Fun
Scrapbooking off the Page…and on
    the Wall
Sculpted Threads
Sew Sentimental
Stitched Collage—*New!*

KNITTING & CROCHET
365 Crochet Stitches a Year:
    Perpetual Calendar
365 Knitting Stitches a Year:
    Perpetual Calendar
A to Z of Knitting
Amigurumi World—*New!*
Crocheted Pursenalities
First Crochet
First Knits
Fun and Funky Crochet
Handknit Skirts
Kitty Knits—*New!*
The Knitter's Book of Finishing
    Techniques
Knitting Circles around Socks
Knitting with Gigi
The Little Box of Crocheted Throws
The Little Box of Knitted Throws
Modern Classics
More Sensational Knitted Socks
Pursenalities
Wrapped in Comfort

Our books are available at bookstores and your favorite craft,
fabric, and yarn retailers. If you don't see the title you're looking for,
visit us at **www.martingale-pub.com** or contact us at:

1-800-426-3126

International: 1-425-483-3313 • **Fax:** 1-425-486-7596 • **Email:** info@martingale-pub.com

12/07